AFGHAN WARS

Other Michael Barthorp books published by Cassell:

BLOOD-RED DESERT SAND: The British Invasions of Egypt and the Sudan 1882-1898

SLOGGING OVER AFRICA: The Boer Wars 1815-1902

THE ZULU WAR: Isandlwana to Ulundi

AFGHAN WARS

AND THE NORTH-WEST FRONTIER
1839–1947

MICHAEL BARTHORP

CASSELL&CO

Cassell
Wellington House, 125 Strand
London WC2R 0BB

First published in Great Britain as *The North-West Frontier* 1982
This edition 2002

British Library Cataloguing-in-Publication Data
A catalogue record for this book is available from the British Library

ISBN 0-304-36294-8

Printed and bound in Slovenia by Mladinska knjiga tiskarna d.d.,
Ljubljana by arrangement
with Prešernova družba d.d.

Contents

Acknowledgements

The publishers gratefully acknowledge the following for permission to reproduce illustrations (figures refer to page numbers).

National Army Museum — all except the following:
Army Museums Ogilby Trust — 39
M. Barthorp Collection — 130, 173 (top)
Anne S. K. Brown Military Collection — 88/9
Gordon Highlanders Museum — Front cover, 86, 87, 131
R. G. Harris Collection — 45
Ray Hutchins — 4–7 (maps)
India Office Library — 77
R. J. Marrion Collection — 130 (top), 137
Military Gallery, Somerset County Museum, Taunton — 34, 44 (top)
Ministry of Defence — 158, 159 (bottom), 160 (top/bottom), 161
Navy and Army Illustrated — 110 (top), 112/13, 124, 125
Northamptonshire Regiment Museum — 133, 171
Denis Quarmby Collection — 75 (top)
Queen's Own Highlanders Museum — 79, 146
Royal Air Force Museum — 159 (top)
Royal Highland Fusiliers Museum — 57 (top), 58 (top), 60, 62

To

R. J. M.

who always responds

Foreword

The military operations to counter Islamic terrorism based in Afghanistan, that began in the autumn of 2001, refocussed attention on a region which, apart from the Soviet invasion of that country in 1979, had become of far less significance than it had once been, particularly to Britain and her Empire.

For some hundred years, over the nineteenth and twentieth centuries, this wild, mountainous territory linking Central and Southern Asia, and peopled by some of the most warlike stock upon earth, exercised the wits and shaped the lives of generations of British politicians and public servants, civil and military, their wives and families, who were concerned in one way or another with the security and stability of one of the most crucial outposts of the British Empire, the North-West Frontier of India. Not only did it feature prominently in the lives of such people, but it also touched the minds of many of their fellow-countrymen at home and indeed of others in the English speaking world: through books and periodicals, be they serious discussions of its problems, memoirs and biographies, military histories, novels or adventure stories for boys; by paintings, engravings and water-colours of its scenery, its people, its epic incidents; as the setting for films, radio programmes and, in more recent times, televisions series and documentaries. Much familiarity with the Frontier, and the men of different races who worked out their lives upon it, has been acquired from the stories and poems of one of England's great men of letters, Rudyard Kipling, even if his own knowledge of it was largely second-hand.

Though it is over fifty years since Britain last held responsibility in this region, her part in recent events may have revived interest in how her troops faced up to those earlier responsibilities on and beyond the Frontier into Afghanistan.

The purpose of this book is to attempt an impression, in words and pictures, of Britain's century-long preoccupation with the Frontier, which ranged in time from the accession of Queen Victoria to the end of World War Two, or in terms of armaments, so much a feature of Frontier life, from the flintlock musket to the atomic bomb. Since Britain's preoccupation was political and military, rather than social and economic, and since the region was always one of the most turbulent of all international boundaries, it follows that the story is inevitably one more of war than of peace. The Frontier was a land of the bullet and the knife, where the British and the martial races of their Indian Empire pitted themselves against the fierce and cunning Pathans, who knew and desired no master, and their near-neighbours, the equally ferocious Afghans. Yet such were the natures of these adversaries that throughout the years of conflict ran a redeeming thread of mutual respect and regard.

Here, then, are these adversaries and the land in which they met, its mountains and forests, its forts and villages, as caught by the camera or the artist. Since photography for much of the period, and in such terrain and conditions, was subject to considerable technical limitations, many of its results lack the spontaneity now within reach of the most amateur cameraman, while others are little more than 'snaps' taken by some enthusiastic bystander. Of the other pictures, some are carefully worked paintings done in a studio, though based on personal observation or the evidence of eyewitnesses, others are mere sketches of a scene or incident made on the spot by a participant which, though of little artistic merit, have an immediacy and truth less apparent in the formal paintings; somewhere between the two are the lithographs which were worked up from the drawings of more gifted observers. Since the brush or pencil afforded greater scope for depicting action and movement than the cameras in use over most of this period, the two types of illustration are complementary in trying to recapture the atmosphere of the times. The text is designed simply to set the scene against which the pictures should be viewed by an outline account of the chief events, issues and personalities. For a more detailed discussion of the subject, there are other works, some of which are listed in the bibliography.

The author must acknowledge a particular debt of gratitude to the books of two men, both authorities on the Frontier, Sir Olaf Caroe and Major-General J. G. Elliott. For assistance with the illustrations, he is indebted to the staffs of the India Office Library and Records, the National Army Museum, the Imperial War Museum, the Royal Air Force Museum, the Army Museums Ogilby Trust, the Anne S. K. Brown Military Collection, and the Museums of the Somerset Light Infantry, The Royal Highland Fusiliers, The Northamptonshire Regiment, The Queen's Own Highlanders (Seaforth and Camerons) and the Gordon Highlanders; also to Douglas Anderson, R. G. Harris and R. J. Marrion. Thanks are also due to Dr T. A. Heathcote for his advice, to Canon W. H. Lummis and Major A. G. H. Moore for information, to Messrs Macdonald and Jane's for help in tracing a picture, and to the London Library for its invaluable service. Lastly, the author must express his gratitude to Colonel Muhammad Afzal Khan and other officers of the Pakistan Army for their hospitality and patient forbearance during the course of a memorable visit to some of the places that feature in these pages.

M. J. B.

Jersey,
Channel Islands
1981
(Revised 2002)

Prologue:
Remnants of an Army

Daybreak, 13 January 1842. An icy wind, blowing straight from the distant peaks of the Hindu Kush, was howling across the snow-covered wastes as a handful of desperate, frozen men staggered down the boulder-strewn track that led to the few hovels of a village. A week before there had been four and a half thousand of them: 700 British soldiers, the remainder Indian sepoys and sowars. The previous evening they had numbered only a hundred odd. Now, after a fearful night of slaughter and panic in the freezing twists and turns of a narrow pass, there were barely 40 men on their feet of whom but half were in any condition to fight. The Indian troops were long gone, butchered, frozen to death, or lost for ever in the grim mountains. Only the British remained, some officers of various regiments, one or two survivors of a Bengal Horse Artillery battery, the rest all from Her Majesty's 44th Regiment of Foot.

The latter had been in India all their service; some may have fought in Burma nearly twenty years before; all had sullenly endured a perilous winter in the savage, explosive city they had recently evacuated. Their spirits had been low, even mutinous, during those precarious months, but that time had been as nothing compared with the harrowing conditions of this last week: the pitiless terrain, the snow, the bitter wind; the corpses of men, women, even children; lack of food, shelter and fuel for fires; and every day the fusillades of musketry from hidden marksmen and the long knives rushing in, hacking, stabbing, slashing among the huddled groups too weak in mind and body to

defend themselves. Only the strongest and stoutest spirits could have survived this far.

Their once brilliant uniforms, the elegant bell-topped shakos, the yellow-faced red coatees, the white cross-belts, so imposing a dress for the parade grounds of home, afforded no comfort or warmth in these desert wastes. Even the long greatcoats of those who still had them were of shoddy material through which the wind cut like razors. Only men fortunate enough to have acquired one of the local sheepskin *poshteens* had some protection against the numbing cold. The ammunition in their pouches was down to a fistful of rounds, and the motions to load and fire them from the heavy muskets were increasingly laborious for weakened men with frostbitten fingers.

Yet somehow the worse things became and the more the numbers dwindled, so the resolution of the survivors not to yield hardened. Mutinous the 44th may have been, but their Colours still flew amid their grievously thinned ranks. If they could but get through this day, its close should bring them to the safety of a fort whose garrison still held out.

But it was not to be. Too soon the tribesmen were massing across the track in front, hovering on the flanks like packs of hungry wolves. In the face of such numbers there could be no way through. Wearily the little band turned aside, clambering up the icy slopes of a rocky hillock, there to withstand as best they could whatever fate awaited them. The officers drew their swords and pistols, the men looked to the flints of their muskets and fixed their bayonets. There was

Tribesmen from Kohistan with long-barrelled jezails wearing their winter costume, circa 1840. Lithograph after James Rattray.

nothing more they could do but wait, huddled close together as much for warmth against the winter wind as for protection from their slowly advancing enemies, their battered boots trampling the snow into slush. No need for orders now, just load and fire, load and fire, until the ammunition ran out or death intervened.

Presently, a party of horsemen detached itself from the oncoming horde and rode up the hill with cries of friendship. Apparently there was to be a truce, a safe conduct would be guaranteed. Let the arms be handed over and all would be well; they could proceed unharmed. But other similar guarantees had been uttered over the past week and those who had put faith in them were now either hostages or corpses. To move a mile without arms in this terrible country was tantamount to suicide. Better a fight to the death among comrades here, than face a tormenting, cat-and-mouse flight down the thirty miles to safety. No, the arms would not be given up.

Impatience ended the argument. Angry hands grabbed at a musket, its owner fired, others followed suit, and the horsemen wheeled away. The die was cast. Grey figures shrouded in cloaks and turbans rushed to a neighbouring hilltop where, invisible among the rocks and crevices, their long-barrelled *jezails* began their deadly task. One by one the little band on the hillock diminished. Their muskets had neither the range nor the accuracy, their targets were concealed, and gradually the remaining rounds in their pouches dwindled. Other figures burst from the boulders below and came screaming up the slopes, the big Khyber knives glinting in upraised hands. The soldiers closed up and met the rush with their bayonets. Once, twice, perhaps more, such onslaughts were thrown back, but in the intervals the firing was renewed and each attack broke on fewer and fewer bayonets.

Above the black shakos the bright Colours still snapped in the wind but, rather than allow such a prize to fall into enemy hands, an officer, Captain Souter, ripped them from their pikes and wrapped their silken folds around his body under his coat. Hardly a round now remained, not a man still on his feet was without a wound from bullet or knife. The dead and dying outnumbered those who stood, back to back, bayonets levelled. On the grey figures came once more, surging upwards from all sides. A quick, savage flurry on the summit, a clash of steel on steel, and it was all over. The tribesmen stood triumphant on the hill of Gandamak.

Six wounded men were made captive, among them Captain Souter, whose brilliant waist covering seemed to betoken a possible hostage of high rank and importance. For the others, their torments were over. The Army of the Indus had ceased to exist.

Later that afternoon, as the garrison at Jalalabad anxiously strained their eyes towards the hills for some sign of the retreating army, a solitary horseman was spied riding slowly towards the fort. From his stumbling progress it was clear that both man and horse were exhausted. As he drew closer he waved his cap at the men on the battlements. Soon it was observed that he wore European clothing and a party went out to bring him in. He was covered in cuts and bruises and in his hand was a broken cavalry sabre. Though at the end of his strength, he managed to announce that he was Dr William Brydon, a medical officer with the army of which he believed he was the sole survivor. Apart from those who had fallen into enemy hands as prisoners, this was indeed the case.

So ended, in total and unmitigated disaster, the beginning of Britain's involvement in one of the most savage and intractable regions upon earth: the mountainous terrain that lies between the Indian sub-continent and Central Asia. During the century that followed, this region would assume great strategic importance as the most vulnerable frontier of British India. In the course of ensuring the security of this frontier, generations of soldiers and administrators, British and Indian, would be faced with the additional problem of the unruly tribes which inhabited it. The harsh and forbidding landscape would witness many scenes of bravery and daring, stupidity and incompetence, selflessness and determination, cruelty and betrayal. For a hundred years this frontier would loom large in the consciousness of the British, assuming a legendary quality which it has never entirely lost to this day.

AFGHANISTAN
AND
THE PUNJAB

IN THE NINETEENTH CENTURY

KEY

———— International Boundary

······· Inner Boundary of N.W. Frontier Province, 1901

+++++ Principal Railways

～～ Rivers

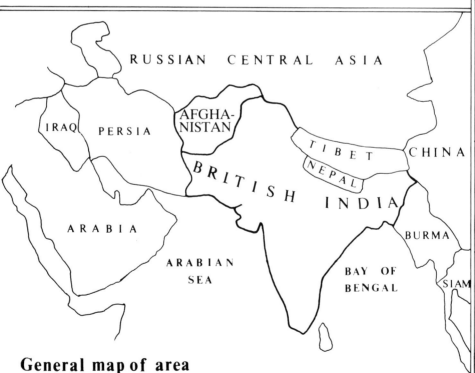 Mountain Ranges

• Principal Cities

General map of area

RUSSIAN CENTRAL ASIA

KIZIL KUM DESERT

KARA KUM DESERT

Khiva

Tepe

AMU DARIA R. (OXUS)

SYR DARIA R. (JAXARTES)

Tashkent

Khokand

Bokhara *Samarkand*

TURKESTAN

Merv

Panjdeh

CHINA

Kashgar

Yarkand

PAMIR MTS.

KARAKORAM MTS.

BADAKHSHAN WAKHAN

Barogil

Balkh

AFGHAN TURKESTAN

HINDU KUSH MTS.

Hunza

Chitral *Gilgil*

INDUS R.

Herat

Kabul

KABUL R.

Peshawar

Srinagar

HIMALAYA MTS.

KASHMIR

LOGAR R.

Khyber P.

Murree

Rawalpindi

Ghazni

KURRAM R.

Jhelum

JHELUM R.

Chillianwala

CHENAB R.

Gujerat

AFGHANISTAN

Kalat-i-Ghilzai

Bannu

Maiwand

GOMAL R.

Dera Ismail Khan

RAVI R.

Lahore

Amritsar

Simla

Ludhiana

JUMNA R.

Kandahar Ft. Sandeman

ZHOB R.

Chaman

Khojak P.

PUNJAB

Ferozepore

SUTLEJ R.

HELMAND R.

Quetta

SULEIMAN MTS.

Multan

Meerut

Bolan P. *Sibi*

Dera Ghazi Khan

Delhi

Kalat

BALUCHISTAN

BRITISH INDIA

Jacobabad
Shikarpur

INDUS R.

Khairpur

SIND

Miani *Mirpur*

Hyderabad

Karachi

ARABIAN SEA

0 50 100 150 200 250 300

MILES

EASTERN AFGHANISTAN
AND THE NORTH WESTERN
FRONTIER PROVINCE

OXUS R.

KUSH MTS.
•Mastuj
CHITRAL
L. Shandur P.

•Chitral

KAFIRISTAN

DIR
YUSUFZAI

LAGHMAN
SWAT
MAMUNDS
Chakdara

BAJAUR
Malakand P.
BUNER •Sitan
•kabul
KABUL R.
MOHMAND
Shabkadr •Malka
Ambela P.
KhurdKabul P.
Jagdalak P.
•Tezeen •Jalalabad
•Marden
Gandamak •Dacca
KHYBER
PESHAWAR
•Nowshera
PESHAWAR •Peshawar
SAFED KOH RANGE
AFRIDI
•Attock
Shutargardan P.
Peiwar Kotal
BARAR
TIRAH
•Bara
Kurram R.
ORAKZAI
Kohat P.
Samana R.
Dargai hts. •Ft. Lockhart
•Kohat
KHOST
BRIT ISH INDIA
Thal
KOHAT
KHATTAK
WAZIR
Miranshah
•Bannu
TOCHI R. •Maizar
BANNU
WAZIRISTAN
WAZIR
•Razmak
MAHSUD
•Wana •Jandola
•Tank
WAZIR
DERA ISMAIL
KHAN
ZHOB R.
GOMAL R.
INDUS R.
BALUCHISTAN •Dera Ismail Khan

AFGHANISTAN
KUNAR R.
PANJKORA R.
SWAT R.
KURRAM R.
KURRAM FORT

KABUL
Sherpur Cantonm
CHARDEH VALLEY
ASMAI HEIGHTS
Kabul
KABUL R.
Ba
Hiss
0   1   2

6

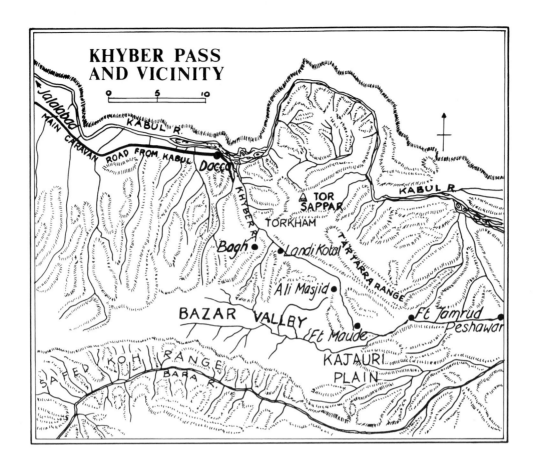

KHYBER PASS AND VICINITY

0   5   10

Jalalabad · MAIN CARAVAN · ROAD FROM KABUL · KABUL R. · Dacca · KHYBER R. · TOR SAPPAR · TORKHAM · KABUL R. · Bagh · Landi Kotal · Ali Masjid · TATTARRA RANGE · BAZAR VALLEY · Ft Maude · Ft Jamrud · Peshawar · KAJAURI PLAIN · SAFED KOH RANGE · BARA R.

KEY

————— International Boundary (Durand line)

- - - - - Inner Boundary of N.W. Frontier Province — post 1901

· · · · · · Administrative Boundary of N.W.F.P.

• Principal Cities

SWAT Provinces & Districts

WAZIR Principal Pathan tal groups

0   25   50   75   100

MILES

1

A Prickly and Untrimmed Hedge

At the north-westerly end of the great Himalayan range lie further groups of mountains, the Karakoram and the Pamirs, with peaks rising from 12,000 to over 20,000 feet. From this junction of soaring uplands another mighty range stretches slightly south of west across northern Afghanistan towards the Persian plateau. Centuries ago slaves brought from the Indian plains were driven north through its passes where thousands perished from the cold, thus giving it its name, the Hindu Kush — Killer of Hindus. To the north its slopes fall away to the desert steppes of Turkestan and Uzbekistan whereon lie the once-mysterious cities of Khiva, Bokhara and Samarkand. Through its passes marched the phalanxes of Alexander the Great, the Mongol hordes of Genghiz Khan and Tamerlane, or Timur Leng. From its eastern end another tangled chain of mountains extends south-west, away from the Hindu Kush until the Kabul river is reached. Between this river and the Kurram further south, the Safed Koh range runs from east to west towards the western extremities of the Hindu Kush. South of the Kurram, the mountains continue their south-west trend, merging into the Suleiman Range which itself falls away southwards to the Sind desert and eventually the Arabian Sea.

Some fifty to 150 miles east of, and roughly parallel to, this 700-mile range of south-westerly mountains flows the River Indus, which rises north of the Himalayas but breaks through them to continue its long course to the sea. Along its left bank are tributaries which also rise in the Himalayas and flow across the plains of northern India,

the fertile Punjab, whose name derives from these five rivers — the Indus itself, the Jhelum, Chenab, Ravi and Sutlej. The tributaries on the right bank rise mainly in the mountains and plateaux of Afghanistan and cut their way through the south-westerly chain which divides them from the Indus. The chief of these is the Kabul river, which itself has two tributaries, the Kunar and the Swat, flowing into it from the north-east, before it joins the Indus at Attock. Further south is the Kurram river, with a tributary of its own on the right bank, the Tochi. To the south again, just below Dera Ismail Khan, is the Gomal, itself fed by the Zhob river flowing roughly north-east from its source east of Quetta in Baluchistan. Close to Attock the Indus drives in a torrent through ravines but then opens out to some 50 yards, widening to about a mile just before the Kurram is reached.

It is this area between the Indus to the east and the westerly exits from the mountains that run parallel to it which has become generally known as the North-West Frontier, although, as will be seen, the term 'frontier' is here used in a geographical, rather than a political, sense.

To the west of this region lies, of course, Afghanistan, itself centred on the Hindu Kush, and bounded on the north by Turkestan, on the west by Persia or Iran, and to the south by Baluchistan. Its eastern gateways to the Punjab lie through five main passes. Due east from the Afghan capital of Kabul, the most famous pass of all, the Khyber, runs parallel to the Kabul river for 35 miles from Landi Khana to Peshawar. To the south the

Typical Frontier terrain with village and watchtower in the foreground.
The photograph was taken circa 1880.

Kurram Valley leads to Thal, from whence routes branch off north-east to Kohat and south-east to Bannu. The latter also lies at the end of the pass through the Tochi valley from the Afghan town of Ghazni, from which another route through the Gomal valley passes to Dera Ismail Khan. Neither the Tochi nor the Gomal routes are as significant as the final gateway to India, the Khojak and Bolan passes which carry a road from Kandahar, the southernmost city of Afghanistan, through Quetta, situated between the two passes, to Sibi at the southerly end of the Suleiman mountains. These are the approaches to India from the west, but far to the north there are routes from the Pamirs through the Baroghil and Killik passes, down through Chitral and Swat, until the Pesha-war valley is reached via the Malakand Pass.

Along this frontier, between the Indus and westwards into Afghanistan, live a warrior race, fierce, cruel, proud and owning no man as master — the Pathans. Basically of Iranian stock, to which over the centuries other strains, Greek, Bactrian, Hunnish, Turkic and Mongol, have been added, the Pathans are of two main branches: those who inhabit the south-westerly parts of Afghanistan, now more commonly called Afghans, and the eastern branch spread across the mountains west of the Indus. Between the two are found the Ghilzais, who are part Pathan and partly of Turkish origin. To the north of the Hindu Kush are another people of Turkish origin, the Uzbegs; to its west are Hazaras, Mongol descendants of the hosts of Genghiz Khan.

9

Tribesmen at Jalalabad about 1879.

The River Indus at Attock with the fort built by the Mughal Emperor Akbar in 1586 on the far bank.

10

The Khyber Pass looking eastwards from Ali Masjid.

The Pathans themselves are divided into tribes which are further divided into clans. There are a great many tribes, some large, some small, but as far as the eastern Pathans along the Frontier are concerned, the following are the most important. From the north, discounting the Chitralis who are not a Pathan people, the lands of Dir, Swat, Buner and the area along the Indus known as the Black Mountain are inhabited by the Yusufzai, a large grouping with many sections and sub-sections. The Yusufzai country contained a number of fertile valleys, unlike some tribal territories, and in Dir and Swat the people gave to their rulers a greater degree of respect and regard than pertained among the more independently minded tribes further south. West of the Yusufzai and north of the Kabul river are the Mohmands, a tough, truculent people, easily inflamed by religious hysteria and ever ready to seize from elsewhere the necessities of life which their own barren countryside did not

permit them to produce. Astride the Khyber and along its length to the Kajuri plain west of Peshawar, and south across the Safed Koh to the Tirah valley is Afridi country. Well armed and formidable, the Afridis were noted for their greed and were as untrustworthy as they were mistrustful of others — including their own kith and kin. Between the Tirah and the Kurram live their neighbour, the Orakzais, fanatical and brave; between them these two tribes could muster the largest force of fighting men on the Frontier. In the Kurram Valley are Turi, who being Shiah Moslems are viewed with suspicion and dislike by their neighbours who are all Sunnis. From Thal southwards to the Gomal river stretches Waziristan, inhabited obviously by Wazirs, but also in its southern region by the Mahsuds with Bhitannis to their east. The latter were relatively placid but the two former were among the most ferocious of all tribes. In his book, *The Pathans*, Sir Olaf Caroe, the last British Gov-

11

The Bala Hissar fort at Peshawar, originally built by the Emperor Babur in 1526 but rebuilt by the Sikhs in 1830.

ernor on the Frontier, likened 'the Mahsud to a wolf, the Wazir to a panther. Both are splendid creatures; the panther is slier, sleeker and has more grace, the wolf-pack is more purposeful, more united and more dangerous'. Eastwards of the Wazirs and reaching north towards Attock are Khatacks, a tribe of greater probity than many others and who in the British era gave loyal and cheerful service when enlisted as soldiers or levies. South of the Gomal, on either side of the Zhob river are a number of tribes of a different strain from those to the north, but still Pathans. Beyond them, however, on the lower reaches of the Frontier, are Baluchis, Brahuis, Marris and Bugtis who are not Pathans but are of more mixed descent, some of Arab stock, some Persian. As will be seen in due course, these latter people, though troublesome enough in their day, were brought under control more quickly than the purely Pathan tribes to the north, most of

whom remained a problem throughout the entire epoch under review here.

Much of the Pathan's combative temperament derives from the code of honour by which he lives — *Pakhtunwali*. This imposes upon him three important obligations which he must observe or face lasting dishonour and ostracism. Fugitives must be offered safety and protection; hospitality must be offered at all times, even to a deadly foe; and any insult, whether it be real, imagined or by default, either to an individual, his family or his clan, must be avenged no matter how long such vengeance takes to accomplish. Such a code — not dissimilar to that once pertaining in the Highlands of Scotland — inevitably encourages a touchy pride, a fiery temper and an easy familiarity with the use of arms. A quarrel, a slight, a theft of *zar, zan* or *zamin* — gold, women or land — and a feud ensues, family against family, clan against clan, even tribe against tribe, until

12

Street scene, Peshawar.

sufficient blood has been spilled to expunge the insult. Such feuds were commonplace among the tribes; the Afridis in particular being so consumed by internal feuds that they had scant time for inter-tribal quarrels. In the case of murder, not only would the murderer's life be forfeit, but frequently also those of his male relatives. Occasionally, when confronted by a common danger or when crops had to be harvested, a truce might be called to suspend a feud, but it was only ever an armistice, not a permanent peace.

An early European traveller was told by the Pathans: 'We are content with discord, we are content with alarms, and we are content with blood; but we will never be content with a master.' Due to their intensely independent and democratic nature, the powers of their headmen, or *maliks*, were slight. Pathan affairs are deliberated by a *jirga* or council, but the more democratic the tribe or other grouping, the larger the *jirga*

with consequent difference of opinions. Though Pathans may not respond readily to authority or any sort of hierarchy, it has always been a different matter where their priests are concerned. Among the most devout of Moslems, they have ever been highly susceptible to the preachings of fanatical mullahs. When such have passed from village to village in the mountains, urging all true believers to rise in a *jehad* — a holy war — against the infidel, this call upon their faith, allied to their deep-rooted desire for independence, has seldom found the tribesmen reluctant to obey. Feuds would be temporarily set aside, the *lashkars* — tribal groupings of armed men — formed, and the heights crowned by natural marksmen, the nullahs and ravines filled with bands of swordsmen, all ready to inflict death, torture and mutilation, or die in the attempt, secure in the knowledge of a place in Paradise. Well have these proud people and their rugged homeland been described by Sir Olaf Caroe

13

as 'a prickly and untrimmed hedge between Rawalpindi and Kabul.'

Many invading armies have passed through the land of the Pathans. Persians, Greeks, Turks, Mongols, they have come from the Iranian Plateau or the wastes of Central Asia, seeking a way through the mountains in search of land, slaves, riches and new kingdoms to conquer on the fertile plains of India. In ancient times Darius the Persian and Alexander the Macedonian made massive endeavours but reached no further than the Indus valley. Tamerlane established a great empire in Central Asia in the fourteenth century and got as far as Delhi. Not until 1528, when the Turk, Babur, came out of Turkestan, drove through the passes and on to Delhi to found the great Mughal Empire stretching from Afghanistan to Calcutta, did any of these invaders achieve anything of lasting permanence. Under

Kohistan tribesmen in summer costume, circa 1840. The jezails and Khyber knife stuck in the waist sash are clearly visible. Lithograph after James Rattray.

Babur's great successors — Akbar, Shah Jehan, Jahangir, Aurungzeb — the inhabitants of what later became Afghanistan and the North-West Frontier were merely subjects of the Mughal Empire, unruly and rebellious subjects though they were. The Frontier area itself became significant only as a region of difficult terrain.

By the eighteenth century Mughal power was beginning to wane. Their Empire had been under pressure at its outer limits in the west for many years, and in 1739 the ruler of Persia, Nadir Shah, led his army into India and attacked Delhi. From sunrise to midday the city was sacked and the inhabitants massacred. In response to a personal appeal by the Mughal Emperor, Nadir Shah stopped the butchery but departed with a vast amount of booty, including the famous Peacock Throne and the Koh-i-Noor diamond, and the cession of all Mughal lands west of the Indus.

Nadir Shah made further conquests north of the Hindu Kush but his increasingly barbaric rule estranged his Persian subjects. To protect his person he employed a Pathan bodyguard, led by one Ahmad Shah of the Abdali clan of the western Pathans. In 1747, while quelling a Kurdish revolt in central Persia, Nadir Shah was murdered by a number of his Persian officers. Arriving too late to save his monarch, Ahmad Shah realised his own life was in jeopardy and therefore rode east with his followers, eventually reaching Kandahar. With the death of Nadir Shah a power vacuum now existed in the country of the Pathans which Ahmad Shah quickly filled. Elected by the Afghans to be their king, he proclaimed himself 'Durr-i-Durran', or Pearl of Pearls, from an earring he habitually wore, and his people, the Abdalis, were henceforth known as the Durranis.

Within nine years he had carved out an Afghan Empire stretching from the Oxus to the Indus, from north-west Persia to Kashmir, and southwards into Baluchistan. In 1756 he looted Delhi. Two years later his eastern provinces were attacked by the Mahratta Confederacy from western and central India but, after defeating the

Pathan fort or watchtower. Water colour by Harry Lumsden, circa 1857.

Mahrattas in 1761, he went on to further enlarge his domains by overcoming the Sikhs at Lahore and even annexing Tibet. Such a vast territory was, however, too extensive to hold, and in due course he returned Delhi to the Mughals and much of the Punjab to the Sikhs.

In 1773 Ahmad Shah died, aged only 50, and was succeeded by his son Timur. Timur sired 23 sons but by the time of his death twenty years later he had failed to nominate one of them as his heir. Anarchy followed until one son, Zaman Shah, seized the throne by the simple expedient of imprisoning his other brothers and starving them until they acknowledged him. However, one of the brothers, Mahmud, had earlier escaped to Herat in the west of the country. From then on, until 1818, Ahmad Shah's great kingdom was rent by struggles for power, first between Zaman and Mahmud, and later, after Mahmud had had Zaman blinded, between Mahmud and a third brother, Shuja-ul-Mulk.

If Mahmud, an idle and vindictive man only rivalled in cruelty by his son, Kamran, proved a more durable ruler than Shuja-ul-Mulk, he owed his power entirely to the abilities of Fateh Khan, chief of the Barakzai, a clan of the Durranis. In 1809, when Shuja-ul-Mulk had temporarily regained the throne, it was Fateh Khan who defeated Shuja's forces in the field and restored Mahmud to the throne. Mahmud re-occupied Kabul and drove Shuja from Peshawar. The latter took refuge with the Maharajah Ranjit Singh, the leader of an increasingly powerful Sikh kingdom centred on Lahore in the Punjab, whose ambitions would inevitably, sooner or later, bring him into conflict with Mahmud's kingdom across the Indus. In 1813 Ranjit Singh seized the

Pathan tribesmen from the Kurram area in the late 1870s. Note the same type of shield as worn by the horseman in the previous illustration.

Shah Shuja-ul-Mulk, Amir of Afghanistan 1802–1809, and from 1839 until murdered in 1842. Lithograph after Vincent Eyre.

The Kohat Pass with, in the foreground, Fort Mackeson named after the first British Commissioner at Peshawar, murdered in 1853. Water colour circa 1878 by Major R. C. W. Mitford.

old Mughal fort at Attock, which guarded the crossing of the Indus, and successfully resisted Fateh Khan's efforts to re-capture it.

Despite the loss of Attock, Fateh Khan remained the mainstay of Mahmud's regime, but his power in the kingdom was incurring the jealousy and enmity of Kamran, Mahmud's son and Governor of Herat. In 1818 Fateh Khan saved Herat from capture by a Persian army, but was refused funds to pay his victorious troops by Kamran. Enraged, Fateh Khan sent his younger brother, Dost Muhammad, to seize what was required from Kamran's palace. In the course of doing so, Dost Muhammad stripped a young woman of her clothes and removed from her person a jewelled girdle. Unfortunately, the girl proved to be Kamran's sister. This rash gesture was Kamran's opportunity to dispose of Fateh Khan. Notwithstanding the latter's years of loyal service to Mahmud, the father would not deny the son his sadistic vengeance. The Barakzai chief was seized, blinded, scalped, flayed and finally had his limbs amputated.

Such base ingratitude and disgusting cruelty inflamed the whole Barakzai clan into rebellion. Mahmud and Kamran were driven from Kabul and Kandahar but reached safety at Herat. Here Mahmud died but Kamran managed to establish a kingdom of his own. Having rid themselves of the Durranis, the twenty-one brothers of Fateh Khan then began to dispute among themselves who should inherit the throne. After eight years plotting and feuding, during which Afghan control of the outer provinces was lost, Dost Muhammad, Fateh Khan's favourite and the most able of the brothers, seized power. However his kingdom was now reduced to little more than Kabul and Ghazni. Another brother ruled in Kandahar, while a third governed Peshawar and the domains west of the Indus as a vassal of Ranjit Singh.

The opportunities afforded by the strife within Afghanistan had not been lost on Ranjit Singh. As formidable a warrior race as the Pathans, the Sikhs were more cohesive and better disciplined. With the aid of European adventurers, veterans of the Napoleonic Wars, Ranjit Singh began to build up a large and well-equipped army, the Khalsa, trained on European lines and particularly strong in artillery. In 1819 he captured Kashmir and occupied the Derajat in the northern Punjab. Four years later he sent his army across the

Jamrud Fort, between Peshawar and the Khyber Pass, built by the Sikh Governor of Peshawar, Hari Singh, in 1823, who was killed here in battle with the Afghans in 1837. The photograph was taken circa 1865.

Indus at Attock for a devastating raid on Peshawar. The trans-Indus region was coming more and more under Sikh domination and, as the former Afghan possessions contracted, so did the mountain ranges and passes between Peshawar and Kabul once again assume the character of a political barrier.

Meanwhile Shuja-ul-Mulk, in exile at Ludhiana in the eastern Punjab, had not given up hope of regaining his kingdom from the Barakzai usurpers. In 1832 the Amirs of Sind offered him free passage through their realms to Kandahar. Ranjit Singh, too, saw advantage for himself in furthering Shuja's ambitions. He would provide men and money for Shuja's enterprise, if in return Peshawar and the trans-Indus region were formally ceded to the Sikh kingdom. Although Peshawar was not actually in Shuja's hands, the latter agreed. In 1834 Shuja's mercenary army occupied Kandahar and was poised to attack Kabul. Before he could do so, Dost Muhammad advanced and utterly defeated him, forcing Shuja to flee west to his nephew, Kamran, at Herat. In an uncharacteristic act of generosity Kamran allowed Shuja, once his father's rival, to return to Ludhiana.

Ranjit Singh, in the meantime, having complied with his side of the bargain, annexed and occupied all the Peshawar area up to the eastern end of the Khyber, throwing out Dost Muhammad's brother and installing a Sikh general, Hari Singh, as Governor. A great fort was built at Jamrud, west of Peshawar, to cover the approaches from the Khyber. The Sikhs now controlled, with a heavy and oppressive hand, all the land between the Indus and the foothills of the North-West Frontier; its freedom-loving Pathan population groaned under the yoke of an occupying power, alien both in race and religion.

For Dost Muhammad this seizure was an affront both to his Islamic faith and his ownership of lands which for a hundred years had been Afghan by right of conquest and which for centuries had been the home of people of his own race. In 1837, therefore, he

Muhammad Akbar Khan, the son of the Amir Dost Muhammad Khan, of Afghanistan. Lithograph after Vincent Eyre.

sent troops under his eldest son, Muhammad Akbar Khan, through the Khyber to attack the Sikhs. Aided by tribesmen, Akbar's army defeated the Sikhs under Hari Singh outside the walls of Jamrud. Though Hari Singh was slain, the Sikhs managed to fall back inside the fort and hold out. Unable to overcome its defences, Akbar raised the siege and retreated back up the Khyber.

Never again would the Afghans hold Peshawar or the trans-Indus lands, and once more the Frontier intervened between Sikh and Afghan. But now other eyes, neither Sikh nor Afghan, were being drawn to its mountain passes. Far away beyond the Hindu Kush columns were on the move, men in green coats or grey, marching beneath standards that bore the double-headed eagle — the blazon of the Russian Tsar. At the same time, to the east, across the Sutlej boundary of the Sikhs, other columns were massing. Some had white faces, others brown, but these wore red coats — the uniform of the Queen of England and her Indian proconsuls. The Great Game was about to begin.

2

John Company

A year after the first Afghan emperor, Ahmad Shah, sacked the Mughal capital, Delhi, in 1756, a huge host of 50,000 men under the Nawab of Bengal, Suraj-ud-Daula, was defeated on the field of Plassey, near Calcutta. The victors were an Anglo-Indian army of only just over 3,000 men under the command of a one-time clerk, Robert Clive, a servant of the Honourable East India Company. By treaty with the Mughal Emperor in 1611, this trading company had begun its operations from a few posts round Bombay and on the Coromandel coast of south-east India. From such humble beginnings the Company prospered mightily, both financially and territorially, at the expense of rival European trading companies and of Indian rulers who, for gain or revenge, had opposed the Company's progress. To secure and defend its gains the Company raised its own troops, largely from the native population, a force which, with its European training and discipline, soon proved itself capable of overcoming Indian armies of vastly superior numbers. Up to and including the Seven Years War, during which Plassey was fought, the Company's chief opponent had been its French equivalent, the Compagnie des Indes. Although France had been predominant in the Indian sub-continent over the first half of the eighteenth century, by the close of the Seven Years War in 1763 its military power had been crushed by the Company's forces.

In the latter half of the century the Company found itself opposed in Bengal by the Mughal Emperor, Shah Alam, and the Nawab of Oudh; in southern India by the Sultan of Mysore; and in the centre and west

by the Mahratta Confederacy. By 1800, when far to the north Ahmad Shah's empire was beginning to disintegrate, the whole of southern India was controlled by the Company, as was Bengal, Behar and Orissa, while the domains of Oudh and Hyderabad were under its protection. The great Mahratta Confederacy, stretching across India from the Bay of Bengal to Gujarat north of Bombay, and from Hyderabad northwards almost to Delhi, took longer to subdue, owing to the pressures elsewhere of the Napoleonic Wars, but by 1819 all its vast territories had passed into the Company's control. All that now remained outside the Company's over-lordship was Sind, astride the lower reaches of the Indus, and the Sikh domains of Ranjit Singh.

The first British contact with Ranjit Singh occurred in 1806 when an army under Lord Lake crossed the Sutlej into Sikh territory in pursuit of the last undefeated Mahratta chief, Holkar, who had taken refuge in the Punjab in the hope of persuading the Afghans to come to his aid. Ranjit had weighed the advantages of throwing in his lot either with the Company or with Holkar. After assessing the military merits of the two opposing armies, he made an agreement with Lord Lake to expel Holkar from the Punjab, in return for which the Company would neither enter his territory nor seize any of his property. Lake allowed Holkar to depart to his own domains and withdrew his own troops to the neighbourhood of Delhi and Agra behind the River Jumna, then the frontier of Company territory.

This was before the days when Ranjit had

built up his army into the formidable force it later became, and the Company could, if it had so wished, have added the Punjab to its possessions without great ado. However its policy at that time was one of consolidation of territory gained, rather than further costly expansion. Moreover Napoleon was then at the height of his power in Europe. A Franco-Persian treaty in 1807, followed in the same year by the alliance signed at Tilsit between the French and Russian Emperors, alerted the British to the possibility of a Franco-Russian advance through the passes of the north-west towards India, as so many other conquerors had done before. In the event of such an undertaking, the Afghan and Sikh kingdoms would provide a useful buffer between the invaders and the Company lands east of the Jumna. A defensive alliance with their rulers against Napoleon was therefore highly desirable and in 1809 envoys arrived at the Afghan and Sikh courts.

The Afghan throne at this time was occupied, albeit briefly, by Shuja-ul-Mulk, who signified his willingness to meet the Company envoy at Peshawar, his winter capital. The latter, the Honourable Mountstuart Elphinstone, a shrewd, compassionate and far-sighted man, thus became the first British official to encounter the Pathans, for whom he conceived a great admiration, sensing that here was a people with whom a bond could be forged. He later wrote a book *Caubul* (a title referring to the Afghan kingdom, rather than the place, which he never visited) that gave to its British readers their first insight into a region with which so many would later become familiar. His discussions with Shuja-ul-Mulk proceeded amicably and fruitfully but before they could be brought to a successful conclusion, Shuja was ousted from power by Mahmud, as already described. Elphinstone therefore had to return to India. His mission had failed but the impression he

British officer and sowars of the Honourable East India Company's 7th Bengal Light Cavalry, circa 1845. Coloured engraving after H. Martens.

Havildar, sepoys and bandsmen of the 65th Bengal Native Infantry in marching order, circa 1845. Coloured engraving after the H. Martens.

had made among the Pathans lingered for many years.

Meanwhile, at Lahore, Ranjit Singh had proved less concerned with global strategy than with absorbing into his kingdom the territory which lay between the Sutlej and the Jumna and which belonged to the Malwa Sikhs, who themselves were seeking British protection against Ranjit. During the very negotiations with the Company's envoy over the anti-French alliance, Ranjit sent his troops across the Sutlej, occupying the towns of the Malwa Sikhs and leaving garrisons therein.

To the British, this sudden aggression, bringing the Sikh power within 60 miles of their outposts, seemed a more immediate threat than the far more distant one of Napoleon, then facing his first set-back in his attempted annexation of Spain and Portugal. Rather than confronting the ambitious and unpredictable Ranjit across the Jumna, it might be wiser to establish a confederacy of friendly Malwa chiefs under British protection, using their territory as a buffer between the Sikh kingdom and British India. Diplomatic pressure, backed by hints of military action, was therefore applied to Ranjit Singh to induce him to withdraw behind the Sutlej. Deeply impressed by what he had seen of the Company's troops, Ranjit eventually agreed. On 25 April 1809 a treaty was signed, whereby he undertook not to interfere further with the Malwa Sikhs, while for its part the Company would respect his territorial rights north of the Sutlej. A British protectorate was established over the disputed territory, from which all Company troops were withdrawn, save for a permanent outpost at Ludhiana, the place to which Shuja-ul-Mulk would come in exile five years later. Foiled in his efforts to expand eastwards, Ranjit Singh seized Kashmir and the former Afghan provinces across the Indus, as described in the last chapter. The Company's western frontier now advanced, for all intents and purposes, from the Jumna to the Sutlej.

The enormous increases to the Company's territories in the early nineteenth century,

Two officers of the Bengal Horse Artillery, in undress and full dress, with European gunners behind, circa 1845. Coloured engraving after H. Martens.

and the administrative and financial burdens they imposed, had caused the authorities in London considerable misgivings. The struggles with France and her Indian allies in the eighteenth century had long ago begun the process of transforming the East India Company from a mere trading concern into a political power on the sub-continent. Its directors in London, alarmed by the diversion of its servants' energies from trade into war and administration, had perpetually tried to limit the territorial expansion. However, forces beyond their control, namely the hostility and bellicosity of a series of Indian rulers, had compelled the Company's servants on the spot to react if the Company's interests were to be protected. By 1784, so important a political power had the Company become in India and so widespread its responsibilities for government, not to mention the fortunes accumulated by some of its servants, that the conduct of its affairs could no longer remain solely in the

A Queen's regiment of Foot on the march in northern India, circa 1840. Behind the Band and Drums rides the colonel with the sergeant-major beside him, followed by the Grenadier Company. All ranks are in undress uniform with covered forage caps, red shell jackets and the light blue cotton trousers issued in India. Part of a water colour panorama by Lieutenant C. Steevens, 28th Regiment.

hands of its Board of Directors. In that year the India Act was passed, so that its operations would be subject to Parliamentary supervision. Henceforth all the Company's political and military activities became the responsibility of a Board of Control in London, whose President was a Parliamentary appointment. The Company itself remained the agency through which British India was governed, its Court of Directors in London providing the link between the Board of Control and the Company's operations in India. All the Company servants, civil and military, were appointed by the Directors; an officer in the Company's army, for example, receiving his commission from the Company and not, as in the case of the King's army, from the Crown.

The possessions in India were divided into three Presidencies: Bengal, Madras and Bombay. Each was independent of the others, with its own civil and military estab-

lishments, and was presided over by a Governor who was directly responsible to the Court of Directors in London. In due course Bengal became the largest and most important Presidency, and in 1774 its Governor was promoted to Governor-General, with powers over the other two Governors in the field of foreign policy and matters affecting the Company's possessions as a whole. After the 1784 Act the post of Governor-General of Bengal (from 1853 styled Governor-General of India) became a Parliamentary appointment. Although hereafter he was obliged to implement the instructions of the Government at home, and his policies and decisions were subject to Government approval or otherwise, he was nevertheless the man on the spot. Furthermore the time taken for despatches to pass between London and Calcutta was so lengthy that much had to be left to his judgement. Not until the opening of the Suez Canal in 1869 and the advent of fast steamers could a reply be received from London in under two months, and the introduction of the telegraph the following year cut communication time to a matter of hours.

However, in the first decade of the nineteenth century, when the then Governor-General, Lord Minto, was confronted by the problem of Ranjit Singh, instructions from London took eight months to reach him. His extension of the Company's authority from the Jumna to the Sutlej may have run contrary to the general policy of consolidation rather than expansion, as indeed the authorities in London pointed out to him, but there was nothing the latter could do about it. A Governor-General who exceeded or failed to carry out instructions from London could of course be recalled or compelled to resign, but the results of his zeal or indolence were almost certainly irretrievable. Minto's predecessor, the Marquis Wellesley, elder brother of the Duke of Wellington, and perhaps the most expansionist and independently-minded Governor-General, did resign after considerable acrimony with London over his actions, but in his seven years of office he transformed the map of India. As far as is known neither Wellesley nor Minto conceived of the mountains of Afghanistan as the ultimate frontier of British India, but it was their policies that launched the Company's armies on a slow but inexorable advance to the north-west.

By the 1830s these armies could pride themselves on nearly a hundred years of almost unqualified military success. The experiment of enlisting the indigenous races and training them to manoeuvre and fight according to European disciplines and evolutions had reflected great credit on the Company's British officers and non-commissioned officers. Years of campaigning and shared experiences had developed deep bonds of loyalty, trust and mutual respect between the officers and their sepoys. However, the passing years and the progression of events northwards had wrought changes in these armies.

The Madras Army, the oldest and once the largest, whose sepoys under Clive and Strin-ger Lawrence had won southern India from the French and overcome the Sultans of Mysore, declined in importance and prestige as events passed beyond the boundaries of its Presidency. In the first quarter of the nineteenth century the Madras Army furnished many troops for the Burma War of 1825, but its prime task, one that would become increasingly more and more uneventful, was the garrisoning of the Presidency. The days of its greatness in the eighteenth century would never come again.

The Bombay Army, the smallest of the three, having played a major part in the Mahratta wars and with important work still before it, did not suffer the same decline as their Madras comrades. It was the Bengal Army which, by virtue of its size and its location on what might be termed the front-line of British India, had become, by 1830, the most prestigious, certainly in its own eyes, both officers and sepoys considering themselves superior to the other two. Whether such self-esteem was merited is questionable, but the Bengal Army certainly differed in one important characteristic — the matter of caste.

The Company had always recruited regardless of a man's religion but since its territories, in the early nineteenth century, were predominantly populated by Hindus, so men of that religion were more numerous in its ranks than Moslems. The Hindu religion imposes many binding obligations and prohibitions upon its believers, whose place in relation to their fellows and every facet of their daily lives are determined by the caste to which each belongs. This is a highly complex grouping system with many sub-divisions but it is a ritual system, rather than a social or hierarchical one; a high-caste man might occupy what to Western eyes might appear as quite a lowly position without affront to his caste. In the army, though this is slightly different, a senior native officer could be of low-caste while the sepoys under his command were high-caste. But the rules governing every aspect of the Hindu's conduct are strict and any man who broke the rules, wittingly or unwittingly, became automatically polluted, expelled from his group, and could only be reinstated after lengthy, expensive ceremonies.

To enlist as soldiers men whose daily lives were so hedged with religious scruples obviously posed delicate problems of discipline and man-management. Caste could not be allowed to interfere with the former, but lack of sensitivity towards it could well impair the latter. In the Madras and Bombay Armies men of all castes served together in the ranks and were promoted for ability regardless of caste, finding their pride and self-respect in their regiments, rather than their caste. The Bengal Army prided itself on its men's appearance and, wishing to assimilate its ranks as much as possible to European troops, looked for tall men with fairer skins than those, say, of the Madras regiments. Such men were to be found in plenty among the high-caste Brahmans and Rajputs from Oudh and Behar, who made fine, upstanding soldierly figures in contrast to the smaller, darker, wirier men of the other armies. Imposing they may have been, and from not too great a distance not that dissimilar to a British regiment, but with such men caste was all-important. The great difference between the Bengal Army and the other two was that in the former caste prejudices were allowed great latitude and, by the 1830s, this was beginning to supervene above military discipline and efficiency.

In the mid-eighteenth century the native regiments had been largely officered by Indians with a couple of European subalterns to guide and supervise, three white NCOs for drill purposes, and from 1766 a European captain in command of a battalion. By 1830 each of a sepoy battalion's ten companies was under a British captain or lieutenant with another British subaltern to assist and two Indian officers, a subedar and a jemadar, who were men risen from the ranks. A similar proportion pertained in cavalry regiments. There were, however, various 'local' and irregular corps in which only the commanding officer, second-in-command and adjutant were British, all other officers being Indian. Whereas in the regular regiments the number of white officers naturally downgraded the Indian officers' prestige and responsibility, the irregular system imposed greater responsibilities on both types, with beneficial results in the way of pay, interest and military competence.

Alongside this lowering of the Indian officers' status in the regular regiments, symptoms were starting to appear of a weakening of the bonds between the British officers and their sepoys, a lessening of sympathy and interest in the latter as individuals, in their way of life and in their motivation. With England less remote in time and with the arrival in India of increasing numbers of English women, the nineteenth century Company officers, particularly the young ones, developed a more European outlook on life than had their forbears of the previous century. Furthermore the rapid spread of the Company's domains and responsibilities threw up large numbers of political and administrative posts which the Company's civil service was not large enough to fill. These afforded new opportunities for advancement to military officers but inevitably they attracted the ambitious and more able officers, leaving the regiments correspondingly the poorer in the quality of those that remained.

In the 1830s these unsatisfactory tendencies in the Company regiments were only just beginning to be revealed, but the consequences of taking the sepoys for granted could be serious, as one officer observed: 'Treat the sepoys well; show that you have confidence in them — prove to them that you look upon them as brave men and faithful soldiers — and they will die for you! But abuse them; neglect them; show an indifference to their wants and comforts — and they are very devils!'

Besides the sowars and sepoys of the native cavalry and infantry, there was another element in the Company armies, known as Europeans but by the nineteenth century almost entirely British and particularly Irish. These were men enlisted by the Company for service in either the one or more wholly white regiments of infantry maintained by each

Alexander Burnes, Lord Auckland's special envoy to the Amir Dost Muhammad in 1837. Lithograph after Vincent Eyre.

Presidency, or in the artillery, both horse and foot. No corps was more typical of these tough, hardened Company Europeans at their best than the Bengal Horse Artillery, a corps d'élite known as 'The Red Men', from the colour of the horse-hair manes streaming from their helmets. Condemned to a lifetime of service in India, the men of the European regiments welcomed the chance of active service 'with an instinctive fierceness and alacrity' as an escape from the tedium of hot, dusty cantonments.

In 1830 the infantry of the Bengal Army stood at one regiment of Europeans and sixty-nine of sepoys, each of one battalion, plus fifteen 'local battalions' which included three of Gurkhas. The Madras and Bombay infantry totalled fifty-one and twenty-six sepoy battalions respectively. The Company cavalry were of two types: the regular regiments of light cavalry, of which Bengal and Madras had eight each and Bombay three,

all being dressed, trained and equipped similarly to British light dragoons; and the irregular, or 'silladar' horse, four in Bengal, one in Bombay, though more would be raised later. The prototypes for the latter were those famous corps raised by two adventurers: the Irish-American, William Gardner, who had fought as a mercenary for a Mahratta chieftain and married an Indian princess, and the half-caste James Skinner, who had raised Skinner's Horse, and who formerly had also been in the Mahratta service.

The military strength of British India was completed by King's or Queen's regiments of cavalry and infantry sent out from England and attached to each of the Presidency armies. By 1835 these numbered four regiments of light cavalry and twenty battalions of infantry. In those days of the long-service soldier, with troopships taking months to reach the East, regiments were faced with long tours of duty in India and British soldiers, like the Company Europeans, could spend their entire service there. For example, the 44th Regiment, which has already been met earlier in this story, arrived in India in 1822 and did not return home until 1843 — and then only as a small cadre. The 16th Lancers, the first British cavalry regiment to be equipped with the lance, were exiled for a similar period. As the ranks wasted from disease, casualties or discharge, so they were filled up by drafts of recruits from home. When a regiment finally left India, men could opt to transfer to their relieving unit; some took their discharges and remained in the country in which they had spent much of their adult lives. In later years, after the Indian Mutiny, the tours of duty were reduced to about a dozen years. Heat and boredom, drink and cholera could rot a regiment in India, but when the call to arms came, unless it was pitchforked into a campaign immediately on its arrival, men would at least be acclimatised and experienced soldiers, well versed in the ways of the country. Royal Artillery detachments had served in India in the eighteenth century, but in the first half of the nineteenth the Company's horse and foot artillery, being predominantly

A Company official who played a leading role in the First Afghan War, Sir William Macnaghten, Chief Secretary to Lord Auckland and Envoy to Shah Shuja-ul-Mulk in 1839. He was murdered, like Burnes, at Kabul in 1841. Lithograph after Vincent Eyre.

European, was relied upon; later, batteries of the Royal Artillery, horse and foot, would return. Engineer services were also provided by the Company's sappers and miners, which too had a sizeable European element.

The King's and Company's regiments were organised, equipped and trained alike. Since the beginning of the nineteenth century, their chief weapons — the sword for the cavalry, the flintlock musket and bayonet for the infantry — had remained unchanged. So had the drills and tactics, the close-order evolutions of squadron or battalion in line or column, providing the shock action of the charge and the fire effect of disciplined volleys. The ordered, steady ranks, the levelled muskets tipped with bayonets, the lines of bright sabres had overcome everything that native India had thrown against them. From Madras to the Sutlej the lines and columns had wheeled and manoeuvred across the level countryside of the sub-continent, shattering the martial reputations of successive warrior hosts. But in 1837, the year of Queen Victoria's accession, a new and still distant terrain, peopled by yet more warriors, of a ferocity and determination greater than any encountered hitherto, was beginning to beckon the red-coated columns ever closer.

3

To Thwart the Tsar

On 19 December 1837 a horseman rode through the narrow streets of Kabul, making his way towards the great citadel of the Bala Hissar which overlooked the bazaars and houses from a commanding height south of the city. Though of foreign appearance, he passed unhindered between the flat-roofed buildings with their latticed shutters overhanging the street, for he came as an envoy from one ruler to another. On reaching his destination he announced himself as Ivan Viktorovich Vitkevich, an officer of Cossacks in the service of His Imperial Majesty, Nicholas I, Tsar of all the Russias, and a bearer of a letter from his sovereign to the Afghan Amir, Dost Muhammad.

The letter expressed little more than the Tsar's courteous hope that friendly diplomatic relations between the two countries might follow from Vitkevich's arrival at Kabul. It was, however, more Vitkevich's presence at his court, rather than the letter's contents, which persuaded Dost Muhammad that here might lie advantage for him, though in a different way from what the Tsar intended. Also in the city at this time was a Captain Alexander Burnes, the special envoy of the Governor-General of Bengal, Lord Auckland, and shortly after Vitkevich's arrival he received from Dost Muhammad a copy of the Russian letter.

Burnes had been an officer in the Bombay Army who had transferred to the political service and whose plausible manner had led to his being selected for a diplomatic mission to Ranjit Singh in 1830. Three years later he acquired far wider fame, and the nickname of 'Bokhara' Burnes, by catching the public imagination with his published account of his travels through Central Asia and Afghanistan, where he had been kindly received by Dost Muhammad. Bold, impulsive, ambitious, his easy charm and linguistic skills were as great an asset to his budding role of diplomat as his notorious reputation as a womaniser was a danger. The good relations he had established with Dost Muhammad on his earlier visit suggested him as a suitable envoy when the Amir sought British aid in his quarrel with the Sikhs over the latter's seizure of Peshawar.

Lord Auckland, who was appointed Governor-General in 1835, was an amiable, courteous man in his fifties who had sat as a Whig MP in the House of Commons since 1810. His administrative ability and conscientiousness had been rewarded by the posts of President of the Board of Trade and First Lord of the Admiralty. He had no knowledge or experience of India or foreign affairs but he was generally considered to be a safe man who as Governor-General would prove biddable, rather than adventurous, where the British Government was concerned. He arrived in India full of decent, liberal intentions for improving the lot of the Company's subjects.

Dost Muhammad's appeal, when it came, seemed to invite meddling in dangerous waters, with the risk of alienating Ranjit Singh, the Company's ally by treaty, and no very obvious return for British interests. Auckland therefore replied that, while he could not interfere in disputes between independent states, he was keen to discuss trade between India and Afghanistan and the development

The Army of the Indus passing through the Bolan Pass at the start of the First Afghan War with tribesmen firing from the heights above. Lithograph after Sir Keith Jackson.

Quetta in about 1840. In the seventies this place was to become an important military centre at the southern end of the Frontier. Lithograph after Sir Keith Jackson.

of the Indus as a waterway for such trade. Burnes was consequently despatched to Kabul with a purely commercial brief.

Arriving in September 1837, he soon became aware that the Amir, whose troops under Akbar Khan had recently returned after their failure to capture Jamrud Fort, was not interested in trade, only in British help to recover Peshawar from the Sikhs. Since Burnes was not empowered to negotiate any political agreements, he could only await further instructions, while amusing himself with the Afghan ladies whom, he wrote, made 'ample amends when indoors for all their sombre exhibitions in public.'

Fresh instructions had in fact been despatched from India just before he arrived at Kabul. Auckland had received a memorandum from the Secret Committee of the Company's Court of Directors who required him 'to watch more closely than has hitherto been attempted the progress of events in Afghanistan and to counteract the progress of Russian influence.' How this was to be done was left to him, but he was empowered to adopt such measures as he thought fit when, in his judgement, it was time 'to interfere decidedly in the affairs of Afghanistan'. Whether Auckland's hitherto blameless, if pedestrian, career qualified him for such freedom of action in a largely unknown and volatile part of the world would be revealed in due course. Certainly the wisdom of entrusting the execution of these orders to a junior officer, ambitious but inexperienced in diplomacy, might have seemed questionable to the Board of Control. Furthermore Burnes' new instructions, as drafted by Sir William Macnaghten, Auckland's Chief Secretary, gave him no real negotiating powers and lacked precision, other than to impress upon him the need to give priority to the interests of Ranjit Singh — a requirement which inevitably placed Burnes at a disadvantage in his dealings with Dost Muhammad.

The origins of the Secret Committee's concern about Russian influence could be traced back to the 1820s, when Russia began to expand down through the Caucasus into north-west Persia. Despite British support

for the Sultan of Turkey as a counter to Russian schemes and diplomatic representation at the Shah's court in Teheran, Russian influence grew until by the early 1830s Persia had become little more than the Tsar's satellite. To make good his losses in the north-west, the Shah was encouraged by the Russians to seize territory in western Afghanistan, notably the state of Herat, still under the cruel but shaky rule of Kamran, whose great-grandfather, Ahmad Shah, had first prised it from the Persian Empire. Persia's first attempt on Herat in 1834 had had to be abandoned, but it had drawn a warning from Lord Palmerston, the British Foreign Secretary, against attacking Afghanistan at the behest of the Tsar.

To Palmerston a Persian-held Herat could provide a base for opening the road to Kandahar, from which Russian armies could strike at India, either via Kabul and the Khyber Pass or south-east through the Bolan Pass. On no account must Russia or a Russian-backed Persia be allowed to establish themselves in Afghanistan. This, where Britain was concerned, was the very essence of the Great Game, the opening moves of which were now being made. The key to preventing such a situation was clearly an Amir in Kabul who was well disposed to British interests. The question beginning to exercise Lord Auckland and his advisers in 1837 was whether Dost Muhammad was such an Amir.

Despite the British Government's warning, the Shah lent a more receptive ear to the Russians and in late July 1837 again set his armies in motion against Herat. On 1 December the siege of Kamran's ramshackle capital began; its resistance was not expected to last long. Eighteen days later the Tsar's envoy to the Amir of Afghanistan arrived at Kabul.

Meanwhile Burnes, armed with his new instructions but hampered in his dealings with Dost Muhammad by his directive that the Sikh interest must have priority, had reported that, although the Amir was friendly towards the British, his chief preoccupation was the recovery of Peshawar. Unless

Auckland was prepared to adjust his policy by coming to some accommodation with the Amir, there was a danger that in desperation Dost Muhammad might turn to the Russians for support against the Sikhs. Furthermore, though the Sikh alliance might appear more advantageous immediately, what would happen when the ageing Ranjit Singh died? When Burnes received from the Amir the copy of the Tsar's letter brought by Vitkevich, this too he forwarded to Auckland as evidence of the Amir's goodwill and stated preference for British, rather than foreign help in furtherance of his cause — exactly as Dost Muhammad had hoped.

However, these representations, and Burnes' continued advocacy over the next three months of Dost Muhammad as a more lasting ally, found less and less response with Auckland and Macnaghten. Apart from offering one slight compromise over Peshawar, which proved totally unacceptable to the Amir, the Governor-General was in-creasingly of the view that the latter was hostile to British interests: he had received a Russian envoy; he had been offered help by Russia and Persia; there were Russians with the Persian army besieging Herat; and he was being unyielding to Britain's ally, Ranjit Singh. Only if he was prepared to reverse his attitude could he expect British friendship. Faced with such obduracy and in need of an ally who might support him against his Sikh enemy, Dost Muhammad turned, in April 1838, to Vitkevich. Burnes' warnings had come true. There was nothing further he could do and he left for India.

Auckland regarded this as fully justifying his distrust of the Amir. Only by his replacement with a new ruler, favourable both to the British and the Sikhs, could Russian influence in Afghanistan be curbed. The most suitable contender seemed to be he who had occupied the Afghan throne in Mountstuart Elphinstone's day — the Shah Shuja-ul-Mulk. Since his abortive attempt to recap-

Men of a European regiment, possibly HM 2nd Foot, at the storming of Ghazni, 23 July 1839. The soldiers are fighting in full dress with black covers to their shakos, the officers are in undress. Engraving after Lieutenant J. Wingate, 2nd Regiment.

The fortress of Ghazni after its capture. The gateway which was stormed can be seen above the party of British infantry in white-covered shakos. At extreme right is a 16th Lancer, on his left a Bengal Horse Artilleryman with a white cover over his helmet. Engraving after Lieutenant J. Wingate, 2nd Regiment.

ture his throne from Dost Muhammad in 1834 he had continued to reside at Ludhiana, now in British territory. His character and suitability had been glowingly reported on by the Company envoy at the Sikh court and this, together with his acceptability to Ranjit Singh and some unsubstantiated reports as to the welcome his restoration would receive in Kabul, was enough to convince Auckland and Macnaghten he was their man. Moreover, since Ranjit Singh stood to gain much from such a change of rule in Kabul, in particular recognition of his right to the trans-Indus lands which had been so disputed by Dost Muhammad, it appeared likely that, provided the British financed the undertaking, Shah Shuja could be re-installed by Sikh bayonets. The effect on the Afghans of having a monarch imposed on them by their hated enemies seems to have been entirely overlooked by Auckland.

It was not, however, lost on Ranjit Singh.

Though apparently all in favour of the plan at first, he had no intention of risking his beloved army in the passes. By shrewd and clever bargaining during his discussions with Macnaghten, he talked the latter into agreeing to commit Company troops to the enterprise, the Sikh contribution gradually reducing to a promise of a stand-by force poised at Peshawar to assist if necessary. This he guaranteed by becoming a signatory to the tripartite Treaty of Simla in June 1838 between himself, Shah Shuja and the British. In return his ownership of the trans-Indus lands was confirmed. Shah Shuja was to be restored to his throne with British help and, once installed, would agree to British control of his foreign policy. Auckland announced his intentions with regard to Afghanistan in a Manifesto on 1 October, which listed the follies of the usurper, Dost Muhammad, and stated that, once Shah Shuja was restored to his rightful throne, the British troops that

31

Kabul and the Bala Hissar at the time of the First Afghan War. Lithograph after Sir Keith Jackson.

The fort at Jalalabad held by Sir Robert Sale's brigade from November 1841 to April 1842. Water colour by G. Thomas, 1847.

had escorted him there as a precaution against foreign intervention would be withdrawn.

The military problems of launching an expedition from the Company territories east of the Sutlej were immense. The shortest route, across the Punjab via Peshawar, was nearly 400 miles and would entail marching the army with all its guns and ponderous baggage train through the Khyber and other passes before Kabul was reached. In any case Ranjit Singh's friendship did not extend to allowing British troops to cross his territory. The only alternative was a much longer route through Baluchistan and the Bolan Pass and on to Kabul via Kandahar, well over thrice the distance but with easier going and the initial stages assisted by the waterways of the Sutlej and the Indus. In the event this was chosen and preparations went ahead to assemble the 'Army of the Indus'.

This was to consist of two unequal divisions. The stronger, from the Bengal Army, mustered five regiments of cavalry, of which one was a Queen's regiment, HM 16th Lancers, and nine of infantry: HM 13th Foot, the Bengal Europeans, and seven of Bengal Native Infantry. In support were a troop of horse artillery and two companies of foot artillery, all European, and two companies of sappers and miners. The Bombay Army provided HM 4th Light Dragoons and two regiments of native cavalry, HM 2nd and 17th Foot, four regiments of Bombay Native Infantry, two companies of foot artillery (European) and one company of sappers and miners. In addition to these two divisions, there was a contingent raised in India for Shah Shuja himself, of two regiments of cavalry, four of infantry and a troop of horse artillery; many of these were transferred from the Company armies including British officers. The Bombay division, under Lieutenant-General Sir John Keane, was to sail from Bombay to Sind to link up with the Bengal division, under Major-General Sir Willoughby Cotton, and Shuja's contingent which were to advance down the Sutlej and Indus. At this juncture Keane would assume command of the whole army, the Bombay

division coming under Major-General Sir William Nott. The expedition was to be accompanied by Sir William Macnaghten, now appointed envoy to Shah Shuja.

Before the great advance could begin, news arrived that might have caused a more far-sighted man than Auckland to ponder the necessity of embarking on such a venture. Contrary to all expectations Herat's defences had continued to resist all the Persian efforts to take it, due largely to the leadership and professional skill of a young Company officer, Lieutenant Eldred Pottinger. In the course of an unofficial spying mission in Afghanistan, he had found himself in Herat when the Persians attacked and took it upon himself to organise the defence. After nine months desultory and fruitless siege operations the Shah of Persia, under diplomatic pressure from the British Government and conscious of Russia now reconsidering the wisdom of its Persian policy, abandoned the attempt and withdrew. With his departure the feared danger of Russian expansion in that area had vanished. The Russian ambassador to the Persian court, who had been largely responsible for the attack on Herat, was recalled to St Petersburg, as was Vitkevich from Kabul. The news about Herat reached Auckland in early November but he was unimpressed. Hell-bent on removing Dost Muhammad, and strengthened in his resolve by the endorsement of his plan by the Board of Control, he ordered the expedition to proceed.

The Bengal division marched from Ferozepore on 10 December and on 19 February 1839 the entire army was on the west bank of the Indus, facing the arid deserts of Baluchistan that lay ahead. No army in India had ever moved without a massive train of followers and baggage animals and the Army of the Indus was no exception. The Bengal division alone, of 9,500 fighting men, had 38,000 followers and 30,000 camels; one officer of the 16th Lancers had forty personal servants with him. Apart from military stores and ammunition there were vast quantities of baggage: officers' kits on a scale quite undiminished from those required in a

Skirmishers of HM 13th Light Infantry during a sortie from Jalalabad to seize livestock, 2 April 1842. The mounted sowars are from Shah Shuja's 2nd Irregular Horse. Detail from a painting by David Cunliffe.

permanent, peacetime cantonment; soldiers knapsacks and blankets; the stores of the regimental contractors and their baggage; food for the fighting men, food for the followers, forage for the animals, water for all. The arrangements for re-supplying such a host were sadly deficient, relying heavily on local purchases by the contractors and living off the land, as had always served adequately in India in the past. As was soon discovered, the harsh terrain of Baluchistan did not support the resources of the fertile Punjab or the Ganges Valley, with consequent hardship, shortages, loss of transport animals and troop horses, and thirst. To these miseries were added frequent harassing attacks by hostile tribes in the Bolan Pass, whose depredations fell mainly on the luckless followers. The army reached Quetta at the end of March but failure to reconnoitre the best

routes caused further delays and losses of stores and transport. For troops dressed in the same heavy shakos and red cloth coatees worn at home the heat was now intense. The horses were so weak that the 16th Lancers had to march on foot, driving their mounts forward with their lances. Nevertheless the whole army was concentrated at Kandahar on 3 May where Shah Shuja was formally crowned — amid the apathy of his subjects. Here the resupply situation eased somewhat, but malaria and dysentery cut a swathe through the ranks.

Kabul was still 325 miles away but a better route offering more forage would be available and, as the road climbed, the heat would be less oppressive. Other than pin-prick attacks by local tribesmen, the march hitherto had been unopposed since Dost Muhammad had posted his best troops to block the Khyber

General Pollock's 'Avenging Army' forcing the Jagdalak Pass, 8 September 1842. Water colour by G. A. Croley, 26th Bengal Native Infantry.

route against the Sikhs, in the belief that they posed the greatest threat to Kabul, and that the British, having installed Shuja in Kandahar, would be more concerned with Herat. However at Ghazni the Kabul road was blocked by a mighty fortress, with walls 70 feet high and surrounded by a moat, held by one of Dost Muhammad's sons, Hyder Khan, and a strong garrison. In the hills on either side of the road waited another son with 5,000 Ghilzai cavalry, ready to exploit any weakness of the advancing British.

On 20 July Keane's skirmishers drove in the enemy outposts in front of Ghazni and the fortress was reconnoitred. The walls were immensely strong and the army's only siege guns had been left at Kandahar. Information from an estranged nephew of the Amir suggested that the fortress might be carried by a surprise attack on the Kabul gate, the only

one which had not been bricked up. Keane decided to adopt this course of action, supported by a demonstration against the fortress' southern face.

Under cover of darkness and the noise of a gale a party of sappers under Lieutenant Durand crept up to the walls just before dawn on 23 July. They were spotted and fired on, but managed to place their explosive charges against the gateway and lit the fuze. At first this appeared to have gone out. Then the gate blew up and the storming party, four companies of the European battalions, rushed forward into the breach. As the noise of battle arose out of the smoke and darkness all was confusion at first. An officer, seeing Afghans still in the gateway, ran back to the main column, also all of the British regiments. Conflicting orders were shouted, confusing the troops and especially the

35

Afghan horsemen. Lithograph after James Rattray.

regimental buglers who transmitted their officers' commands. Then, it is said, Bugler Luke White of the 13th, when ordered to sound 'Retire', exclaimed, 'Retire? The 13th don't know it!' and blew the 'Advance'. The infantry surged forward with fixed bayonets. Fierce hand-to-hand fighting ensued in the streets until all resistance was finally overcome and the Union Jack flew from the citadel.

The fall of Ghazni had wide-ranging repercussions. When the news reached Kabul, Dost Muhammad recalled Akbar Khan and his troops from the Khyber to defend the capital. A combined Anglo-Sikh force from Peshawar advanced up the pass unopposed. Dost Muhammad tried to rally his followers to oppose Keane's advance but they melted away before the onward march of the conquerors of Ghazni. The Amir had no choice but to flee northwards, covered by Akbar's cavalry. On 6 August the Army of the Indus entered Kabul, followed a day later by Shah Shuja, come to reclaim the throne he had not occupied for thirty years. Auckland's grand design had taken ten months to accomplish but, considering the hazards and difficulties his men had faced, casualties had been relatively light and many of those had derived from sickness.

With a friendly monarch installed at Kabul, Keane returned to India with the Bombay division and the cavalry, leaving Cotton in command and Nott with a garrison to hold Kandahar. Although it was one thing to put Shah Shuja back on his throne, the unsettled state of the country and the lack of enthusiasm of the Afghans for their new Amir soon made it apparent that he could only be kept there by British bayonets. In the spring of 1840 a cantonment was constructed just outside the city and the garrison settled into the peacetime routine they had known in India. Some officers sent for their families, others discovered the charms of the Afghan ladies, doubtless on the recommendation of Burnes, who was now Macnaghten's assistant. Since women occupied a subordinate place in Pathan society, and since the sexual preference of many males lay with their own sex, the Kabuli ladies were not averse to the attentions of the foreigners. Nevertheless their menfolk observed these goings-on with hatred in their watchful eyes; whatever their personal inclinations, theft of their women was an affront that could only be assuaged with blood. On the whole though, the year passed quietly but for two incidents. In July

36

came news that Russia had again been on the march, this time with an expedition to Khiva, 700 miles to the north-west beyond the Hindu Kush, but this had foundered in the deserts. Then, in November, Dost Muhammad suddenly returned to Kabul where he gave himself up quietly to Macnaghten who sent him down to India.

Although Shuja's regime was neither popular nor efficient, the country continued calm in 1841 due mainly to the subsidies paid by the Company to sweeten the outlying chiefs. However, the rising costs of the Afghan adventure were now causing concern both in London and Calcutta. As an economy measure, therefore, Macnaghten reduced the subsidies and sent Sir Robert Sale's brigade back down the Khyber to India. Enraged by the cut in their subsidy the Ghilzai chiefs east of Kabul attacked Sale in the narrow Khoord-Kabul pass. The brigade, which included Sale's own regiment, HM 13th, had to fight its way through, losing over 100 men, and took refuge in the fort at Jalalabad.

Events now began to deteriorate rapidly. In late October an outpost of Shah Shuja's troops with British officers was massacred by tribesmen north of Kabul in Kohistan. On 2 November Burnes' house in Kabul was surrounded and set on fire by a mob among whom, it was said, were many men who had been personally outraged by Burnes' amorous activities. In the ensuing rioting Burnes, his brother and another officer were murdered.

Had firm military action been taken immediately all might have been well. But Cotton had returned to India some months before and command of the garrison was now in the faltering and reluctant hands of Major-General Elphinstone, an elderly, gout-ridden officer who had seen no action since Waterloo. The news of Burnes' death threw Elphinstone into a jelly of indecision, which his contemptuous second-in-command, Brigadier Shelton, did nothing to resolve. Eventually Macnaghten ordered Shelton to occupy the Bala Hissar, intending to overawe the mobs, but the rioting increased in fury, and two days later a fort holding all the garrison's commissariat stores was isolated from the cantonment, which now held rations for only two days.

Attacks on the British increased with gathering momentum as tribesmen joined

A picquet of the 26th Bengal Native Infantry in action at Tezin, 12 September 1842. Some of the sepoys have removed their European trousers for ease of movement. Contemporary pen and ink drawing.

the mobs from outside Kabul. Elphinstone, weak and ill, handed over command to Shelton, who was recalled from the Bala Hissar. The cantonment, two miles in perimeter, was overlooked all round by high ground which was quickly occupied by the Afghans. Shelton's decisions were constantly questioned by a nervous Elphinstone and, though not without courage, he lacked tactical ability. He bungled his attempts to dislodge the Afghans; the Hindu sepoys, already of low morale from cold and hunger and appalled by the fearfulness of this alien place, hung back; and HM 44th Foot, of which he was Colonel, refused to obey orders. Only the Bengal Horse Artillery came out of these abortive operations with credit. The indomitable Lady Sale, who had remained at Kabul when her husband had left for the Khyber, was equally contemptuous of both European and Indian soldiery: 'They all ran away as fast as they could,' she wrote after one action. 'There was not a pin to choose between them — all cowards alike!'

At the end of November Macnaghten began negotiating with the Afghans, now led by Dost Muhammad's son, Akbar Khan. By 11 December it was agreed that the British should begin to withdrew from Kabul on the 15th under safe conduct. Although the Bala Hissar was evacuated on that day, thus leaving Shah Shuja to fend for himself, the problems of preparing the garrison, together with its women, children and sick, for a winter march through difficult and dangerous country delayed departure. The Afghans come back with more demands while Macnaghten temporised, convinced that, by playing upon their greed and self-interest, he could divide them. His ploys proved his undoing, for at a meeting with Akbar on 23 December to discuss fresh terms, the latter ordered him to be seized and killed. Any trust there might have been between the two sides was now gone forever. The offer of safe-conduct through the passes was made conditional upon European hostages being handed over. Elphinstone was paralysed by events, his every order being followed by a counter-order, every decision questioned by

bitter and angry officers. Surrounded as they were by menace on all sides, the lack of a firm hand at the top spread its effect like a debilitating disease throughout the whole force, from the officers down to the lowly sweepers and grass-cutters. All the while the few remaining supplies dwindled and the weather grew more severe.

At last, on 6 January 1842, the garrison straggled out of Kabul and headed for the snow covered mountains; 700 Europeans of HM 44th and the Horse Artillery, 3,800 Indian sepoys and sowars, the European women and children, and 12,000 half-starved, frozen and terrified followers. The sick and wounded had to be left to the mercy of the Afghans. In the intense cold, with the command and staff arrangements broken down, subject to constant harassing attacks by plundering Ghilzais, all order was soon lost. At night thousands perished from lack of food and fuel, and in the mornings many awoke with frostbite. The panic-stricken followers broke up such ordered formations as the troops were able to maintain, the sepoy regiments disintegrated, and Akbar Khan's promise of an escort proved either false or ineffective as the ambushes and sniping increased. On the other hand his undertaking to protect those Europeans with wives and children if they came to his camp was honoured.

By 10 January only Elphinstone's staff, some 100 sowars, and the remains of the Horse Artillery and the 44th, whom adversity had somehow restored to discipline, remained as a formed body. That night Akbar invited Elphinstone and Shelton to his camp to explain his difficulties with the ferocious Ghilzais, but once there he held them prisoner. When it was clear they would not be returning, the survivors struggled forward again. After a terrible night's fighting in the confines of the Jagdalak Pass, the few that remained came in sight of the village of Gandamak where, on 13 January, the end came, as has already been seen.

Meanwhile at Jalalabad, where the army's sole European survivor, Dr Brydon, arrived later that day, Sale had been holding firm

Four soldiers of HM 31st Foot driving tribesmen away from a wounded officer and sergeant at Mazeema during Pollock's campaign. Lithograph after H. Martens.

since November with his force of HM 13th, the 35th Bengal Native Infantry, a squadron of the 5th Bengal Light Cavalry, a troop of Shah Shuja's Irregular Horse, and some gunners and sappers. His first task had been to disperse local tribesmen who had begun to close in, and then repair the fortifications which were in a parlous state. A number of attacks were successfully resisted in November-December, but in February, following the loss of the army, Akbar Khan arrived to invest the town. An earthquake on the 19th caused great damage to the rebuilt defences but fortunately also interfered with Akbar's operations. Sale had heard that he could expect no relief from Peshawar for some months so he had no option but to hold on. He conducted an energetic defence, mounting sorties to attack the enemy siege works and capture livestock and forage. In early April, having heard a rumour that General Pollock's relief column from Peshawar had been held up in the Khyber, he decided to make a major sortie in the hope that this might assist Pollock's advance. At dawn on 7 April he launched the 13th and 35th NI in

three columns at the Afghan camp, two miles west of Jalalabad. By 7 am Akbar was in full retreat, his guns were taken and his camp burnt. None returned to trouble Jalalabad further. Nine days later, after a siege of 155 days, Pollock's troops marched in, as the 13th's band played the Jacobite air, 'Oh! But ye've been lang a 'coming'. The 13th, later the Somerset Light Infantry, were hailed as 'The Illustrious Garrison' and were awarded the additional title of 'Prince Albert's', together with the badge of a Mural Crown, representing the walls they had defended for so long, superscribed with the name 'Jalalabad'.

The despatch of Pollock's force had been one of the first acts of a new Governor-General, Lord Ellenborough, who had arrived in India in February 1842 to replace Auckland. Though the Kabul garrison had perished and that of Ghazni had been made prisoner, other troops still held out at Kalat-i-Gilzai, on the road to Kandahar, and at Kandahar itself, besides that at Jalalabad. Ellenborough was determined to withdraw fully from Afghanistan but not before these

A Queen's regiment, followed by a sepoy battalion attacking Istalif village, Kohistan after Pollock's occupation of Kabul. Note skirmishers of both battalions on the attacking column's left flank. Water colour by G. A. Croley, 26th BNI.

besieged garrisons had been relieved and British prestige, humbled for the first time ever in the East, had been restored. A force of 8,000 was assembled at Peshawar under Pollock, formerly of the Bengal Artillery, and a capable and experienced officer. His troops included HM 3rd Light Dragoons and 9th Foot, later reinforced by the 31st Foot, two and a half regiments of Bengal Cavalry and six of Bengal Infantry. On 5 April he attacked the Afghans holding the Khyber Pass.

This was the first sight British soldiers had had of a place with which many would later become familiar. An officer of the 9th wrote: 'Every eminence, every crag shelters an enemy. Such a warfare is calculated to try, to its utmost stretch, the fortitude of man. We are all in the highest spirits . . . every man seems to be embued with a spirit of adventure.' Such a warfare was also an entirely new experience for the Company's armies, but Pollock, having studied his enemy and their terrain, appreciated that he must com-

mand and hold the heights, if the main body with its guns and baggage train was to pass unscathed through the gorges. Surprised by their tactics being used against them, the Afghans were driven gradually from their positions till the way to Jalalabad was clear.

Nott, meanwhile, had been reinforced at Kandahar which enabled him to relieve Kalat-i-Gilzai in May. Ellenborough now wished both generals to withdraw, but both reported that no move could be made until sufficient baggage animals had been collected. This was true but it was also prevarication on their part as both were convinced that British prestige would not be fully restored until British troops decisively defeated the Afghans and were seen again in Kabul. There was, in any case, the question of Elphinstone and the other hostages still in Afghan hands. Thwarted by his generals in the field and under pressure from London, whence the Duke of Wellington, himself an old India hand, was urging upon him 'the importance of the Restoration of Reputation in the East', Ellenborough at last gave in and in late July ordered Pollock to advance on Kabul; at the same time Nott was told to evacuate Kandahar but that he could return to India via Kabul if he wished.

Nott's Bombay troops advanced on 10 August. Having inflicted a convincing defeat on the enemy at Ghazni, they entered Kabul on 17 September to find that Pollock had arrived two days before. The latter, joined by Sale's brigade, had left Jalalabad on 20 August. His troops' blood was up for their route took them over ground still littered with grisly remains of Elphinstone's ill-fated column. Though the advance was fiercely disputed by Akbar's troops at the Jagdalak and Tezin passes, Pollock's skill in mountain warfare inflicted heavy casualties on the Afghans with minimum losses to his own men. Realising that he could not repeat January's cat-and-mouse game with this column, Akbar's resistance dwindled to a few hit-and-run attacks before he withdrew northwards, leaving the road to Kabul open.

The Grand Bazaar of Kabul was burned in retribution for Macnaghten's murder and a punitive expedition was led by Sale into Kohistan. As for the hostages, it was found that Akbar had been as good as his word, despite his defeats in the field; apart from Elphinstone, who had died in captivity, all were alive and well. Their release was a moving experience for all concerned; even the stout-hearted Lady Sale, whose spirits had remained undaunted by the harrowing retreat and the months of captivity, was moved to tears by the welcome she received from the ordinary soldiers of her husband's 13th Light Infantry. The unfortunate Shah Shuja had been murdered the previous April. One of his sons now sat uneasily on the throne but with Akbar Khan still at large the situation was by no means stable. However Pollock was under orders not to interfere

politically and on 12 October 'the Avenging Army' marched out of Kabul, heading for Peshawar. Nott's rearguard came under attack several times in the passes but no serious resistance was encountered. Two days before Christmas 1842 the troops reached British India at Ferozepore.

Although the reputation of British arms had been restored, the destruction of Elphinstone's army left an indelible impression on the minds of men from Kabul to Calcutta. John Company, hitherto invincible, was proved to be fallible after all. Furthermore, within the Company's armies, particularly that of Bengal, the conduct and sufferings of some of the sepoy regiments raised doubts and misgivings among both their British officers and the sepoys themselves; the mutual trust, so essential for cohesion, had taken a hard knock.

Politically Auckland's great undertaking had been a failure. It is true that no soldiers of the Tsar had emerged from the Bolan or massed at the gates of the Khyber to threaten India. That this was so was due, not to the unfortunate Shah Shuja, nor to the Company bayonets which had propped him on his precarious throne, but to diplomatic exchanges in far-off London and St Petersburg. All that had been achieved, at enormous cost in blood and treasure, was the instillation in Afghan minds of feelings of hostility, distrust and resentment towards the British — the precise opposite to what Auckland had hoped to accomplish. The folly and waste of it all was finally demonstrated in January 1843 when Dost Muhammad returned with British blessing to his throne. There he would reign quietly for another 20 years and by his actions prove that Burnes' assessment of him had been right and Auckland's wrong. Not only would no Russian disturb the peace of his country, but in British India's darkest hour he would be found a true and loyal friend.

4

Across The Indus

Within seven years of Pollock's troops debouching from the Khyber after their successful campaign, the Company would be back in the disputed Peshawar province, this time to make the North-West Frontier the ultimate boundary of British India. Before that occurred, however, the focus of events shifted much further south, to the flat, mainly desert lands astride the lower reaches of the Indus and the hilly region to the west—Sind and Baluchistan or Kalat.

The population of Sind included Sindhis, Hindus and Baluchis, the latter being the dominant race. It was divided into three amirates: Upper Sind or Khairpur, Lower Sind or Hyderabad,* and Mirpur. Each was a masterpiece of misgovernment, the Amirs motivated solely by self-interest and self-indulgence, keeping the mass of their people cowed by bands of Baluchi horsemen. The mountains west of Sind were populated by Brahuis and other Baluchi tribes — Marris, Bugtis and Domkis. These people formed a loosely-knit confederacy under the Khan of Kalat. The importance of these lands in the eyes of the East India Company was their geographical position astride the route from Karachi, up the Indus, through the Bolan Pass to Kandahar. The Company had gained from the Amirs of Sind the right to use the Indus for trade in 1831. Seven years later, on the pretext of supporting the Amirs against a claim by Ranjit Singh to Shikarpur in Upper Sind, a treaty had been extracted from them which, by their acceptance of a British Resident, effectively gave the Company control of

*Not to be confused with the other Hyderabad in southern India.

their foreign policy. As has been seen, this secured the safe passage of the Army of the Indus in 1839. It had not, however, endeared the Company to the Amirs. As for the Khan of Kalat, his refusal in 1839 to acknowledge Shah Shuja as overlord had led to an assault on his fortress by a brigade of the Bombay division during which he was killed. He was replaced by another, more pliable claimant.

Despite the treaty with the Amirs of Sind, and the complete withdrawal of troops from Afghanistan, Lord Ellenborough was unconvinced that the Amirs were sufficiently well-disposed to the Company. There seemed, too, little doubt that their people laboured under a terrible tyranny, which perhaps should be replaced by the just rule of the Company. He therefore placed the whole problem of Sind in the capable and ruthless hands of General Sir Charles Napier.

Napier, a man of eccentric appearance, a hero of the Peninsular War and one of a famous family of brothers, was then aged 60. Notwithstanding his age, he had unbounded energy, great speed of thought and, unusual for generals of that era, a tremendous rapport with his soldiers. When in command of the Northern District in England during the Chartist troubles he had kept order and prevented armed insurrection with a firm but just hand, always displaying sympathy and fair-mindedness in an explosive situation. The Amirs of Sind, on the other hand, were a different matter altogether, and if evidence of their hostility had to be fabricated to justify action against them, then the end justified the means. 'We have no right to seize Sind,' he wrote, 'yet we shall do so, and a very

Gen. Sir Charles Napier, conqueror of Sind 1842–43, and later C-in-C, India. Early photograph, circa 1848.

advantageous, humane and useful piece of rascality it will be.'

By requiring the Amirs' agreement to a new treaty, he induced them to take measures for their self-defence, which he then interpreted as preparations to attack him. The overt act of hostility he needed to justify military action against them did not occur until February 1843 when the British Residency at Hyderabad was attacked. Though he mustered only 2,600 troops of the Bombay Army, which included a single Queen's regiment, HM 22nd Foot, he marched against the Amirs and their host of 20,000 Baluchis, utterly routing them after two hard-fought battles at Miani and Hyderabad. Triumphant, he is alleged to have telegraphed his conquest to Ellenborough with his famous, punning signal — *'Peccavi'* (I have sinned).

The Company formally annexed Sind in March 1843, thus for the first time bringing its western boundary across the Indus and adjacent to the southernmost mountains of the North-West Frontier. Napier was appointed Governor and, never sparing himself despite the intense heat, plunged into the task of establishing law, order and just administration, stating as his guiding principle: 'The great receipt for quieting a country is a good thrashing first and great kindness afterwards.'

Napier's subordinates were all military officers, and their incorruptability, common sense and devotion to duty gained them the respect of the hitherto downtrodden inhabitants, whose lot could not but improve. Where Napier's rule was less successful was on the western borders of Sind, where a stretch of desert intervened between the hills wherein lived marauding bands of Bugtis and Marris who would descend into British territory, plundering and burning the villages. Forts with small garrisons of sepoys were built along the border to deter the raiders, but to little avail. Not only were they ineffective, but service in them was deleterious to the sepoys, especially those from Oudh for whom service across the Indus was an affront to their caste. Furthermore, since Sind was now British territory, they were denied the 'batta', or special allowance due to sepoys outside India, which they had been paid in Afghanistan.

So bad did the depredations become that in 1845 Napier led a punitive expedition against the Bugtis, the first of many that would follow up and down the length of the Frontier. It failed to crush them, however, and in December 1846 1,500 Bugtis raided 75 miles deep into Company territory, carrying off 15,000 head of cattle. The situation did not improve until January 1847 when there arrived in Upper Sind a remarkable man who may be described as the first of the great Frontier figures — Major John Jacob of the Sind Irregular Horse.

Born in 1812, the son of a Somerset vicar, Jacob was commissioned from Addiscombe, the Company's Sandhurst, into the Bombay Artillery. After some years with his battery he was employed by the civil authorities in an engineering post in the Bombay Presidency.

Men of HM 13th Light Infantry in action against Baluchi tribesmen on the heights of Truckee, 8 March 1845, during Napier's pacification of Sind. Painting by David Cunliffe.

Returning to military duties he was appointed in 1841 to be Commandant of the Sind Irregular Horse, a 'silladar' regiment which had been raised three years before. Having by now been both gunner and engineer, he soon displayed his talents as a light cavalry leader in the Miani campaign. He acquired a profound understanding of his sowars and, with a judicious mixture of tact and firmness, allowed no caste considerations to interfere with the workings of his regiment, where promotion was entirely on merit and which he brought to a high standard of efficiency. Of great physical and moral courage and endowed with tireless stamina and dedication, he was also afflicted by a pronounced stammer which, he said, had 'a crushing effect' on him. He felt that, without this disability, 'I could force my way

Left: John Jacob, Commandant of the Sind Irregular Horse and Political Commissioner for Upper Sind. Appointed Commissioner for the whole of Sind in 1855.

to anything; as it is, I frequently wish I could hide myself in the earth.' It led him to shun society, particularly that of women, and this, together with the grief he displayed at the forthcoming marriage of a highly-favoured subaltern, have suggested a homosexual nature, though Jacob himself maintained his affection and regard for the young man were those of a father for his son.

On coming to Sind he was made Political Commissioner for Upper Sind with total civil and military power. He commanded the troops, he was superintendent of police, chief magistrate, engineer and revenue officer. Raising a second regiment of Sind Horse, he first set about pacifying his territory. He gave up the forts with their static garrisons and instituted a vigorous, co-ordinated programme of patrolling up and down the desert. Formerly the marauders had been able to slip past the forts at will or even attack them. Soon they grew to fear the tracks of the cavalry patrols, always varied but renewed daily, spreading all over the desert and up into the foothills out of British territory. 'Wherever a party of the Sind Horse came upon any of the plunderers,' Jacob wrote, 'it always fell on them at once, charging any number, however superior, without the smallest hesitation. Against such sudden attacks, the robber horsemen never attempted a stand; they always fled at once, frequently sustaining heavy loss in men and never succeeding in obtaining any plunder.' With only two regiments of irregular horse and his rapidly spreading reputation as a resolute but fair man, he pacified an area the size of England and Wales.

Having made the land safe, he began to irrigate and cultivate it, and then opened it up by building roads and bridges. The little desert town of Khangur, where he established his headquarters, he turned into a flourishing centre, later renamed Jacobabad, surrounded by a fertile area of 100 square miles, watered by a canal from the Indus. Before long the inhabitants, who for years had gone in fear for their lives and homes, were farming and moving about freely, unarmed. By 1854 he could report, with jus-

A British officer of the Sind Irregular Horse in fighting costume, 1849. The officer has a red puggaree round his helmet and a poshteen over dark green jacket and breeches. Lithograph after Ensign Sitwell, 31st Bengal NI.

tification, 'peace, plenty and security everywhere prevail in a district where formerly all was terror and disorder.' In the same year he negotiated a treaty with the Khan of Kalat who, in return for a subsidy, agreed to prevent his tribesmen raiding into Sind.

In addition to all his other work, he found time to invent a clock and a new rifle, he raised two infantry regiments armed with this rifle, and wrote numerous books, pamphlets and papers; in one of these, written in 1850, he forecast the trouble that would erupt in the Bengal Army seven years ahead, for which he was censured. He was appointed Commissioner for the whole of Sind in 1855 with the rank of major-general, and died on 5 December 1858 at the early age of 46, worn out in mind and body by his constant, devoted endeavours.

One factor that had worked in Jacob's favour was that the Baluchi tribes, though warlike and predatory, had a natural respect for and obedience to their chiefs. Once a chief had been won over, his people would generally follow his lead. This was very different from the Pathans at the northern end of the Frontier, whose democratic spirit permitted little acknowledgement of a chief's authority,

45

Major John Nicholson in 1851 — one of the most famous Frontier figures, both as a soldier and an official.

which often carried less weight than the urgings of the mullahs. It was with these intractable people that the soldiers and the administrators of the Bengal Presidency were to find themselves faced from 1846.

Ranjit Singh had never lived to see the outcome of Auckland's policy in Afghanistan. With his death in 1839 the value to the Company of the Sikh alliance crumbled, as Burnes had once predicted. In default of a strong successor, the Sikh court became prey to palace feuds, plots and assassinations. The Sikh army became turbulent and aggressive, on the one hand contemptuous of the Company's defeat in Afghanistan, on the other alarmed by its conquest of Sind. Certain that the Punjab would be next, the Sikhs determined to strike first and in 1845 swept across the Sutlej, confident of victory. A force from the Bengal Army under Sir Hugh Gough checked the advance in two hard-fought battles at Mudki and Ferozeshah, though at terrible cost. In early 1846 Sir Harry Smith won another victory at Aliwal, and three weeks later Gough attacked the main Sikh army entrenched with its back to the Sutlej at Sobraon. This battle, and indeed all those

against the Sikhs, was of a scale and ferocity the like of which British troops had not experienced since Waterloo and the Bengal sepoys never before. Consequently, the brunt of the fighting fell upon the Queen's regiments and two Gurkha battalions, but by the end of the day the Sikhs were routed and Gough's army advanced to occupy their capital, Lahore.

There were those who thought the Punjab should now have been annexed, but the new Governor-General, Sir Henry Hardinge, decided to allow the Sikhs their independence but under British protection, with a nine-year-old boy, Duleep Singh, a supposed son of Ranjit Singh, on the throne, supervised by a British Resident at Lahore. All Sikh territory between the Sutlej and Beas rivers was to be ceded to the Company, the Sikh army reduced in numbers, and British garrisons were to be stationed at certain key points within the Punjab, among them Peshawar.

Appointed to the Residency at Lahore was Henry Lawrence, a former captain in the Bengal Artillery. To assist him in the difficult work of restoring sound administration he

A Pathan malik, or headman, Muhammad Khan. Water colour by Captain W. Fane, circa 1860.

A water colour sketch by Harry Lumsden, founder of the Guides, of his men skirmishing in 1852. All are wearing the khaki clothing made famous by this regiment. The group on the right are interrogating a prisoner.

collected a band of helpers, whom he later described as 'men such as you will seldom see anywhere, but when collected together worth double and treble the number taken at haphazard. Each was a good man, the most were excellent officers.' Among them were names which would later become famous — Lawrence's brothers, John and George, James Abbott, Herbert Edwardes, John Nicholson, Reynell Taylor, William Hodson. Since the Sikh territories extended to the foothills of the mountains west of the Indus, it was these men who first confronted the anarchic conditions resulting from the Sikhs' failure to tame the Pathan tribes. Only at Peshawar had any sort of order or law been maintained by the governor, the colourful and ruthless Italian soldier of fortune, Avitabile, 'whose criminal code was blood for blood, whose object was the sacrifice of a victim rather than the punishment of a culprit.' With nothing but the power of their own forceful personalities, and for military support the same Sikh troops against whom they had lately been fighting, Lawrence's men set about the task of acquainting themselves with the tribes and terrain along the border.

The first Company official at Peshawar was George Lawrence, to whom was posted as assistant a 25-year-old lieutenant of the 59th Bengal Native Infantry, Harry Lumsden. In view of the still uncertain loyalties of the Sikh troops, Lumsden was instructed to raise a special corps whose object, in his own words, 'was to have trustworthy men who could at a moment's notice act as guides to troops in the field and collect intelligence beyond as well as within the border.' This was the regiment, part cavalry, part infantry, which in due course would become one of the most renowned in the Indian Army — Queen Victoria's Own Corps of Guides.* Initially the Corps had only one troop of horse and two companies of infantry, recruited from what Lumsden called 'downcountrymen and Persians' but during his tours of the hills he soon began to enlist Pathans. In time the Guides would include, besides all types of Pathans, Sikhs, Gurkhas, Punjabi Mussulmans (Moslems) and Hindus, Dogras, even Turcomans, and the competition to join would be intense. Lumsden cared neither about their religion, nor their background, seeking out 'the men notorious for desperate deeds, leaders in forays,

*The designation 'Queen's Own' was not granted until 1876.

HM 32nd Foot fighting in the streets of Multan during the Second Sikh War, which led to the annexation of the Punjab in 1849. Lithograph after Surgeon Dunlop, 32nd Foot.

who kept the passes into the hills and lived amid inaccessible rocks'. Only a man of Lumsden's courage, powers of leadership and insight into human character could have welded such wild, warlike and varied material into a disciplined body where no man questioned his authority. In the early days the Guides wore their own clothes dyed to a mud colour, but when, after a few years, they were properly uniformed, a similar colour was chosen for their clothing. Thus they became the first corps in the British or Indian service to adopt a uniform of the shade subsequently known as khaki, from the Persian word *khak*, meaning dust. From their first formation the Guides soon acquired a reputation for daring, dependability and, due to Lumsden's prestige, fidelity.

There was soon other work for the Guides and the British officers on the Frontier, for in April 1848 the Sikhs rebelled against the Company's protectorate. Hearing that the city of Multan had risen in revolt after murdering two British officers, Herbert Edwardes assembled a body of Pathans and rode south to invest it until regular troops could arrive. John Nicholson rode post-haste from Peshawar to try to secure the Indus crossing at Attock. These men and the Lawrences all acted with great energy, but without any regular troops, and the Sikh armies reforming between them and the main Company forces in the eastern Punjab, there was little they could do without reinforcement. The Sikhs took over Peshawar, promising its return to Afghanistan in return for aid.

A division of Queen's and Company troops reached Edwardes before Multan in late August but the city resisted all attempts to take it until early January 1849. Meanwhile Gough had assembled a field army and crossed the Chenab. On 13 January he fought an appallingly costly battle against the main Sikh forces at Chillianwallah. The Sikhs retreated but were still unbeaten and were now joined by an Afghan contingent. With the timely arrival of the division from Multan, Gough felt strong enough to resume his offensive. On 21 February he attacked the combined Sikh and Afghan forces at Gujerat where he at last won a decisive victory. By the end of the day his enemies were routed and in full retreat.

The second Sikh War was over and on 30 March the entire Punjab was annexed by the Company. Some 80,000 square miles were added to British India, whose western boundary now marched with the mountain ranges, from Sind to the Hindu Kush. The problems of the North-West Frontier, as it had now become, were finally in British hands.

5

Masterly Inactivity

The trans-Indus territory taken over from the Sikhs by the British ended at the foothills; no attempt was made to advance into the mountains or even secure the passes. For years the mutual hatred between Sikhs and Pathans, and the rudimentary and unsympathetic administration of the former, had prevented any chance of peaceful development in this region. When the Company assumed full responsibility in 1849 for what became known as the administered districts, the inhabitants' recollections of the fair but firm dealings by Lawrence's men in the two years between the Sikh Wars must have made the new regime seem preferable to the years of Sikh misrule. However, the hill tribes, over whom the Sikhs had never achieved any domination, saw no reason whatever to discontinue the age-old practice of raiding and plundering into the fertile lowlands for their sustenance, indeed they may have welcomed the chance to pit their strength and wits against the new masters below them. Almost at once, therefore, before they had time to assess the problem fully, the British were forced into taking reprisals to impress upon the Pathans their own strength and determination.

The Punjab was administered from Lahore by a Board, consisting of its President, Henry Lawrence, and two members, one of whom was his brother John. Both Lawrences were extremely able, incorruptible, dedicated men, but where Henry was warm and idealistic, John was cold, pragmatic and bureaucratic. Thus they seldom agreed on any issue and after four years Henry resigned, leaving John in sole charge of the Punjab as Chief Commissioner, a title changed in 1859 to Lieutenant-Governor. Also at Lahore was the Chief Court where, in common with the other inhabitants of the Punjab, the Frontier tribes were, in Sir Olaf Caroe's words, 'expected to bring a society which sought redress through the blood-feud within the smug formalisms of the British Indian law.' The frontier area of the Lahore administration was divided into six districts, from north to south: Hazara,* Peshawar, Kohat, Bannu, Dera Ismail Khan and Dera Ghazi Khan. Each district was under a deputy-commissioner, most of whom had been soldiers before they became administrators, and all were outstanding in their different ways and knew the Frontier from their work in 1846–48: men like the kindly, approachable Herbert Edwardes, who believed in winning men by trust, and his counterpart and friend, the brooding, implacable John Nicholson, whose name and reputation made all men — British, Indian and Pathan — fear or reverence him, sometimes both. The aims of the authorities were to protect their subjects in the administered territory from attacks by marauders, to keep the trade routes open, and to maintain peace and order along the border. Although conditions in Sind had lent themselves to Napier's policy of a thrashing followed by kindness, this would and could not be implemented on the northern frontier. It was too long, too mountainous and with too many tribes to be controlled by military action alone, so the

*A cis-Indus district, not to be confused with the Hazara in Central Afghanistan mentioned in Chapter 1.

'Guard, turn out!' A water colour sketch by Harry Lumsden showing a British sentry attacked at night by tribesmen, circa 1852.

policy adopted was one of conciliation, backed by the threat of force if necessary.

Sadly, the Pathans were not a conciliatory people, bitterly resenting the slightest interference with their way of life and quick to exploit anything they regarded as weakness. Between 1846–48 British officials had found that the tribesmen had best responded to a man-to-man approach; by devoting time and patience to their problems it had been possible to win their confidence, or at least make a start. After annexation, however, the bureaucratic work involved in setting up and running the administration of a district allowed far less opportunity for such close contact. In any case no British official was permitted to cross into tribal territory, where the root of all trouble lay, and all discussion had to be carried out through middlemen who were frequently motivated by self-interest, if not malice. Consequently potential trouble, which might have been averted

Indian officers and sowar, the 4th Cavalry, Punjab Irregular Force, Kohat, 1855. Water colour, W. Carpenter.

2nd Cavalry, Punjab Irregular Force, 1856. From left: Hindustani sowar, Sikh NCO, Afghan officer. Engraving after Captain W. Fane.

by direct contact, often exploded before it could be nipped in the bud.

To provide military backing for the administrators, forts were erected along the border and, using the Guides as a model, a special force was raised from Sikhs, Pathans, Punjabi Mussulmans and Gurkhas; these were a very different type of man from the Hindu sepoys of the Bengal Army. Formed in 1849, the Punjab Irregular, later Frontier, Force consisted initially of five regiments of Punjab Cavalry, three mountain batteries, and five battalions of Punjab Infantry. The Sind Camel Corps, raised in 1843, was later converted into the 6th Punjab Infantry. In 1851 there were added four battalions of Sikh Infantry and in 1858 the 5th Gurkha Rifles. The Guides, tripled in strength, were included from the beginning, giving the whole force a total strength of 11,000. Officers were selected with great care from the Company

armies and among them were names which became famous in Frontier lore — Dighton Probyn, Sam Browne (the inventor of the famous belt), Coke, Wilde, Daly, Vaughan. In 1854 its overall command was given to Major Neville Chamberlain, 'that glorious soldier' as Lumsden called him, experienced in the Afghan and Sikh Wars, liked and respected by all who knew him. This force was quite separate from the other Company armies, being directly under the control of the Punjab administration and outside the jurisdiction of the Commander-in-Chief, India.

Since the Punjab Irregular Force had some 700 miles of frontier to guard, support for it was provided by the regular troops, Queen's and Company's, of the Peshawar division of the Bengal Army, whose area also included Attock, Rawalpindi, Jhelum and Murree. By 1852 this was the largest and most important

Officers and men of the 1st Infantry (Coke's Rifles), Punjab Irregular Force, circa 1860. Lithograph after Captain W. Fane.

command in India. Its first commander was Sir Colin Campbell, later Lord Clyde, who laid out the military cantonment at Peshawar, which in time would become familiar to generations of soldiers. Conscious of its proximity to the border Campbell confined the troops into as small an area as possible, with guards and sentries all round the perimeter, and picquets on the approaches. No officers were allowed to go about unarmed and movement beyond the perimeter after dark was forbidden. Even movement by day was dangerous. An officer of HM 98th Foot was mortally wounded when he and a lady were attacked in broad daylight almost within sight of the nearest guard post. The lady escaped but a few nights later an attempt was made to abduct her for fear she might identify a man arrested on suspicion of being one of the officer's assailants. Life at Peshawar in those early days could be precarious: the

need to be constantly watchful, its unhealthiness due to the overcrowding and poor water supply, the sense of danger never far away. It had its compensations on the other hand: crisp, invigorating weather in the winter months, the distant view of the magnificent hills and, for the enthusiastic, ambitious soldier, the ever-present chance of distinguishing oneself on a frontier expedition.

An unruly tribe was brought to heel, if only temporarily, by the imposition of a fine as compensation for property stolen or lives lost. If not paid, the tribe might be blockaded which, by the nature of the country, was difficult to enforce. If all else failed, a punitive expedition was sent against it. Between 1849 and 1857 fifteen expeditions had to be mounted all along the Frontier, from the Baizais of the Swat Valley and the cis-Indus Yusufzais of the Black Mountain in the north, down through Mohmand and Afridi country, to the Wazirs and Shiranis round Dera Ghazi Khan in the south. Some were fairly small, involving only units of the Punjab Irregular Force; others required support from Queen's and Company troops, like Campbell's punishment of the Utman Khel in 1852 which involved four cavalry regiments, six infantry battalions, including HM 32nd Foot, together with gunners and sappers. The first expedition in which Queen's regiments took part was against the Baizais in 1849 at which detachments of HM 60th Rifles and the 61st Foot were present.

Bound up with the question of tribal control was the defence of the Frontier against external aggression. A potential invader of India from the north-west faced two natural obstacles: the mountain ranges between Afghanistan and the Punjab, and the River Indus itself. However, since the Company boundary ran along the eastern foothills of the former, the major part of that obstacle was not in British territory. To be effective as a line of defence, the defenders should hold the western entrances to the passes, but troops deployed there would not only be in Afghan territory, their lines of communication through the passes would be vulnerable to the mountain tribes who, theoretically, were the Amir's subjects. To secure such an obstacle for its use, the Government of India would therefore be compelled to annex it. With the fiasco of the Afghan War still fresh in men's minds, such an undertaking, which came to be known as the 'forward policy', had few supporters in the fifties, though it would be different later. Another school of thought maintained that to antagonise the Afghans by such a policy would be sheer folly; far better to allow an invading army to be mauled in the passes by the tribes who would be resentful of any intruder, after which any that did get through could be easily held on the line of the Indus. This view, the 'close-border policy', was not shared by all military men, including no less an authority than the Duke of Wellington, then in the closing years of his life; its opponents called it 'masterly inactivity'. However, the Russian threat now seemed

An Afridi sepoy, Sikh havildar and Afghan officer of the 4th Infantry, Punjab Irregular Force, circa 1860. All the Punjab infantry wore drab uniforms except for the 1st who had rifle-green. Lithograph after Captain W. Fane.

less real to many, although it re-arose briefly in 1854 when the Crimean War broke out — needlessly as it happened, since Russia's pre-occupations in the West precluded any simultaneous advance in Central Asia. After the war it would again loom large, as will be seen in due course.

In the meantime there was still the question of what, if anything, should be done about the Amir of Afghanistan. Dost Muhammad had little cause to love the British who now occupied the trans-Indus provinces he still regarded as rightfully his, and who were frequently in arms against his Pathan subjects along the Frontier. John Lawrence, the architect and chief protagonist of the close-border policy, took the view that the less the Indian Government had to do with Dost Muhammad the better, an opinion not shared by all his subordinates. Herbert Edwardes was convinced that the time was ripe for an understanding with the Amir and

No 1 Punjab Irregular Battery at Kohat, circa 1860.

argued his case with the Governor-General, Lord Dalhousie. The latter, alarmed by the renewed Russian threat in 1854, eventually agreed that Edwardes might sound out the Amir.

In the event the initiative came from Dost Muhammad who found himself in need of friends when Persia again laid claim to Herat. In 1855 a treaty was signed by which the Company undertook to make no claims on Afghan territory, Afghanistan would recognise the Company's tenure of the trans-Indus province, and each signatory would be 'the friend of its friends, and the enemy of its enemies'. The following year Persia occupied Herat and Britain promptly declared war, sending an expeditionary force from India to the Persian Gulf which forced the Shah to capitulate. In 1857 Dost Muhammad came in person to Peshawar to ratify the treaty, saying 'having made an alliance with the British Government, I will keep it faithfully to death'. That he was as good as his word he proved beyond all doubt when in May the sepoys of the Bengal Army mutinied and the fate of all northern India hung in the balance.

This is not the place to discuss at length the causes and events of the Sepoy Mutiny. A few perceptive men had observed the deterioration in the Bengal Army since the Afghan and Sikh Wars: the growth of mistrust between officers and men, the disillusion caused by the withdrawal of 'batta' from Bengal regiments garrisoning the annexed provinces of Sind and the Punjab, the fears of the caste-ridden sepoys about what seemed to them to be attacks on their religion, and finally the spark that ignited the whole combustible mass — the famous affair of the 'unclean' cartridges. Sadly, the perception of the few was not shared by the many, with the result that the outbreak came like a thunderbolt from a tranquil sky.

With Afghanistan to the west, conflagration to the east, and surrounded by the highly volatile Pathans, the Punjab, and particularly the Frontier, was in dire peril. Fortunately, Dost Muhammad kept his word and the Frontier had men like Nicholson and Edwardes whom a crisis fired into a superhuman energy. In addition there was a greater concentration of Queen's troops in the Peshawar area than elsewhere in India. With these Nicholson immediately disarmed or dispersed potentially mutinous Bengal regiments, to the dismayed protestations of their trusting colonels, one of whom blew his brains out at the disgrace inflicted on his beloved, but rebellious sepoys.

Nicholson's plan for ensuring the security of the Punjab hinged on his belief that, by capitalising on the hatred of the Moslems for the Hindus, and on the Sikhs' desire for revenge on the Bengal sepoys who had defeated them (or at least had been on the winning side) in 1846 and 1848, he could raise sufficient fresh troops from the Punjab

Cricket match on the parade-ground at Kohat, circa 1864.

to overcome the mutineers. Until this could be done, he formed a Moveable Column, at first entirely of Queen's regiments, to deal rapidly with any outbreaks of trouble in the Punjab. At first the call for Pathan and Punjabi volunteers produced disappointing results — all were waiting to see which way the tide would turn — but when it was observed with what speed and ruthlessness Nicholson acted at Peshawar, Nowshera, Mardan and elsewhere, recruits began to flock in.

So effective was the action taken on the Frontier and also in the cis-Indus Punjab by Neville Chamberlain, that when the sorely-pressed British besieging Delhi begged John Lawrence for more troops, he was able to send down regiments from the Punjab Irregular Force, whose loyalty had never wavered; the Guides added to their laurels by a famous forced march to cover the 600 miles between Mardan and Delhi in 27 days, going straight into action on their arrival. Two months later the Moveable Column, now under Nicholson's personal command, arrived at Delhi, bringing not only its seasoned troops, but also the dominating personality of its commander, which lifted the flagging morale of the besiegers and poured fresh energy into the prosecution of the siege. More than anyone it was Nicholson who urged the tired commander of the Delhi Force into making the assault which carried the city, and in which he himself was mortally wounded. His tirelessness, his determination, his speed of thought and action had contributed much to the saving of the Frontier and the Punjab, and the same qualities helped bring the siege of Delhi to a successful conclusion, which marked the beginning of the end for the mutineers all over India.

John Nicholson was 34 years old when he died. The future Lord Roberts, writing 40 years later, remarked: 'Nicholson impressed me more profoundly than any man I had ever met before, or have ever met since.' When the wild, ferocious warriors of the Multani Horse came to pay their last respects to their dying leader, they stood around his deathbed with tears in their eyes. It was the exertions of men like them, and thousands of others from the north-west, brown and white, which saved northern India in the Mutiny, but they neither could nor would have done it had it not been for the leadership and personal example of men such as Nicholson, Edwardes, Chamberlain, the great Frontier figures. Nor could it have been done if Dost Muhammad had not kept his word. Roberts, who as a junior staff officer witnessed all the events from the moment news of the Mutiny reached Peshawar, wrote afterwards that, had the Amir taken advantage of the Company's peril, 'I do not see how any part of the country north of Bengal could have been saved.'

55

6

With War Drum Beating

After the Mutiny British India was greatly changed. The Company rule was abolished and the country henceforth governed directly by the Crown through a Secretary of State for India with his own department, the India Office. The Company Court of Directors was replaced by a Council of India which advised the Secretary of State. In India the three Presidencies continued, each under its own Governor, but with the Governor of Bengal still exercising responsibility for the country as a whole as Governor-General. He too was advised by a Council with Members who were the heads of separate departments of the Government of India: home affairs, the law, finance and military matters; foreign policy and its department was the responsibility of the Governor-General himself.

In the Army too there were changes. The three Presidency armies were retained but the Company Europeans were transferred to the British, or Queen's service, either as part of the Royal Artillery and Royal Engineers or as new regiments of foot. The Bombay and Madras Armies had been almost entirely unaffected by the Mutiny, but the Bengal Army had to be completely reconstituted. Though its regiments continued to bear the title 'Bengal', its men, with very few exceptions, were no longer the Hindus from Oudh and Rohilkand who had betrayed their salt, but men from what came to be known as 'the martial classes', men from the north, Sikhs, Jats, Dogras, Punjabi Mussulmans, Pathans, Baluchis and Gurkhas — the men who had proved their worth as loyal soldiers in the Mutiny. As the century progressed, Indian regiments were recruited more and more from such men, until even the Madras regiments were largely filled with Punjabis.

In parallel with the civil hierarchy, each Army had its own commander-in-chief, the C-in-C Bengal also ranking as Commander-in-Chief India, with a place on the Governor-General's Council as an Extraordinary Member. As such he exercised control over all troops in India, British and Indian, with the exception of the Punjab Irregular Force, re-styled Punjab Frontier Force from 1865. This came under the direct control of the Lieutenant-Governor of the Punjab, who was responsible for it to the Governor-General's Foreign Department. Although in time of war its troops could be placed at the disposal of the C-in-C India, in peacetime its separateness from other troops of the Bengal Army, who might be serving alongside it, made for an anomalous command arrangement. This would not be rectified until 1886 when the Frontier Force was incorporated into the Bengal Army, though retaining much of its distinctive character. The Sind Frontier Force, on the other hand, was controlled by the Commander-in-Chief, Bombay.

No sooner had the Punjab Frontier Force reverted to its proper role after the Mutiny than it was again in action, punishing the Wazirs in late 1859 and the Mahsuds the following year. However the chief trouble in the post-Mutiny period arose, not on the border itself, but in a mountainous region some 40 miles north of Attock, where dwelt a sect known to the British as the Hindustani Fanatics, but to the Pathans as 'Mujhaddin' — Warriors of God. They had

'Eagle's Nest Picquet — A quiet day.' One of a set of eyewitness sketches made by Captain Howard, 71st Highland Light Infantry, during the Ambela Expedition of 1863. He notes, 'men with sprigs of fir in cap were best shots of Regiment'. See next illustration.

The best shots of the 71st HLI, with the fir sprigs in their bonnets and wearing the red serge frocks and tartan trews in which they fought at Ambela. Photograph taken at Peshawar after the Regiment's return from Ambela.

A sketch by Captain Howard showing the 5th Gurkhas repulsing and pursuing the enemy at Ambela on 30 October 1863.

The terrain at Ambela with a picquet position in the foreground.

originated from Hindustan, or Bengal, where their founder, Ahmad Shah, a Moslem from Oudh had ridden with the Pindari robber bands in the second decade of the century. After attracting a following from the Moslems of Bengal by his religious piety, he and his followers fought the Sikhs and eventually settled at Sitana on the west bank of the Indus, just south of the Black Mountain among the Bunerwals in the Yusufzai country. Ahmad Shah was killed by the Sikhs in 1831, but his followers remained at Sitana.

In 1857 they were joined by sepoys of the 55th Bengal Infantry who had mutinied at Mardan and were fleeing from the vengeance of John Nicholson. Sitana became a rallying point for mutineers and others on the run, and with these reinforcements the fanatics began to raid and plunder in the name of religion. Expeditions were sent against them in 1857 and 1858 but, though Sitana was burned, without lasting results. In 1860 the fanatics were raiding again, across the Indus into Hazara, from a new base at Malka, only ten miles from their old one. At the same time they built up an underground organisation all across northern India, with a headquarters at Patna in Bihar, to subvert British rule and draw fresh recruits from the Bengal Moslems. So dangerous did they become that in 1863 a major campaign was mounted to root them out once and for all.

For this, the largest yet undertaken in the north-west, a force of some 5,000 men under Sir Neville Chamberlain was assembled: 100 sabres each of the 11th Bengal Cavalry and the Guides; HM 71st Highland Light Infantry and 101st Royal Bengal Fusiliers (formerly Bengal Europeans); six battalions of the Frontier Force, including the Guides Infantry and the 5th Gurkhas; two of Bengal Infantry; one of Sikh Pioneers; two mountain batteries, a light field battery, one Royal Artillery battery and sappers.

In order to prevent the fanatics escaping into the hills to the north, it was planned to get round behind Malka by advancing through the Ambela Pass into the Chamla Valley, and then driving the enemy southeast towards the Indus, where they would be confronted by another force. The plan depended on the neutrality of the Bunerwal tribesmen north of Ambela, who were believed to have little love for the fanatics. In an attempt to preserve secrecy of the plan for as long as possible, the Bunerwals were not informed of the intended passage through Ambela until 19 October, the day before the pass was entered. Unfortunately, they had already been alerted by the fanatics who called upon them to rise up in defence of their lands which 'the deceitful and treacherous infidels' were coming to plunder and devastate. Thus, by 22 October when Chamberlain's force was fully in the pass, where the going proved far worse than anticipated, he found himself opposed, not only by the fanatics, but by the Bunerwals as well, massing on his left, or northern flank. Any attempt to follow the original plan of swinging south to attack the fanatics' stronghold or even move forward into the Chamla Valley would imperil his rear and his line of communications through the Ambela Pass. Moreover, it was soon learned that, following appeals made by the Bunerwals to the Akhond of Swat, who exercised great religious influence over the tribes to the north-west of Ambela, further reinforcements were on their way from as far off as Dir and Bajaur. Confronted by overwhelming numbers which might reach up to 25,000 tribesmen, Chamberlain realised that he had no option but to hold firm in the pass and wear down the enemy by an attrition process until more troops could reach him; this could take a month or more.

On the north side of the pass a series of ridges climbed to the Guru mountain, 5,000 feet high. On the south side was a lower range of hills which formed the northern slopes of the Mahabun mountain. Pine forests covered much of the slopes but with rocky outcrops and small plateaux thrusting above the trees. To guard the fortified camp in the pass below, picquets were posted on these eminences protected by stone-built 'sangars'. Some were quite small, held by only a dozen men, others contained a company or more. Owing to the broken nature of the ground and the trees, the fields of fire of these picquets were very limited but the approaches to them were covered by the mountain guns from the camp.

It was for the possession of these picquet positions, particularly the Eagle's Nest on the north flank and the Crag on the southern side, that the fiercest fighting ensued by day and night. 'Fortified by prayer and promises of paradise, with war drum beating and shrill pipe screeching', hordes of enemy swordsmen would gather under cover while their matchlock-men poured fire into the sangars, until the moment came to surge forward and plant their standards on the ramparts. Once they broke from cover they suffered heavily from the rifles of the infantry defenders and the supporting artillery fire, but their sheer weight of numbers was often overwhelming. If a picquet was overrun or forced to withdraw, a counter-attack was mounted immediately to re-take it.

A concerted attack was made in the early hours of 30 October when the Crag picquet, then held by only twelve men of Keyes' 1st Punjab Infantry, had to be abandoned in the face of an overwhelming onslaught by the fanatics. As soon as it was daylight Keyes led a spirited counter-attack supported by Brownlow's 20th Punjabis which restored the position. Meanwhile, a breastwork which guarded the eastern end of the pass was attacked by the Swatis, who were held at bay by the 71st and 101st and then charged by the 5th Gurkhas, 'who followed the enemy some distance, ripping open and beheading their victims with their kukries'. Thereafter the Crag picquet was enlarged to hold 160 men and two mountain guns.

A few nights later the tribes attacked at night, as an eyewitness described: 'Suddenly comes a wild shout of Allah! Allah! The matchlocks flash and crack from the shadows of the trees; there is a glitter of whirling sword-blades, and a mob of dusky figures rush across the open space and charge almost up to the bayonets. Then comes a flash and a roar, the grape and canister dash up the stones at close range. The whole line lights up with the fitful flashes of a sharp file-fire, and as the smoke clears off the assailants are nowhere to be seen.' These attacks continued all night but on this occasion each was

'Griffin's Battery — making Umbeyla pegs.' The latter were a rudimentary form of hand-grenade made from soda-water bottles. Some of the 71st in this Howard sketch wear bonnets, others helmets with red puggarees.

Troops at Ambela including, from left, a Gurkha, sepoys of the 3rd Sikhs, British officers of various regiments.

thrown back by the 20th Punjabis. However, on 13 November the position was overrun in broad daylight and the whole of the 101st Fusiliers had to be launched up the slopes to retake it.

Never a day or night went by without skirmishing from the tribes. Chamberlain had begun the construction of two roads, one forwards to Ambela village, the other to provide a better line of communication to the rear over the lower slopes of the Mahabun mountain. All this work had to be protected by covering parties. When the latter was completed, Chamberlain abandoned his positions on the north of the pass, concentrating his whole force on the south side in a new camp which was occupied on 18 November in the face of heavy enemy attacks, at a cost of 118 killed and wounded. Two days later the Crag picquet was lost for the third time but was re-taken the same day by the 71st, supported by the 5th Gurkhas. So im-

portant was this counter-attack that Chamberlain accompanied it in person, only to be badly wounded, which forced him to hand over command to Major-General Garvock who arrived with reinforcements on 30 November.

The Bunerwals, who had lost heavily, were now ready to come to terms; rather than see the British occupy their territory, they offered to destroy the fanatics' stronghold at Malka. However, the Akhond of Swat had just received 6,000 men from Dir, all eager for a fight. Chamberlain had been reinforced earlier by the 4th Gurkhas and 14th Sikhs, and with the arrival of HM 7th Royal Fusiliers and 93rd Highlanders, the 3rd Sikhs and 23rd Pioneers brought in by Garvock, there were now sixteen battalions at Ambela. Garvock therefore decided to go over to the offensive by attacking large concentrations of tribesmen around a prominent conical hill and the village of Lalu to the south-east.

The Crag Picquet at Ambela. In the foreground Howard shows the padre of the 71st with an enemy standard taken at Lalu on 15 December.

At daybreak on 15 December two columns went forward against the conical hill, covered by the Peshawar Mountain Battery. When the 'Advance' was sounded, '5,000 men rose up from their cover, and with loud cheers and volleys of musketry, rushed to the assault — Pathans, Sikhs and Goorkhas all vieing with the English soldiers as to who should first reach the enemy. It took but a few seconds to cross the open ground, and then the steep ascent began, our men having to climb from rock to rock. Foremost could be distinguished the scarlet uniforms of the 101st Fusiliers which steadily breasted the mountain and captured the defences at the point of the bayonet, the enemy's standards dropping as their outworks fell. Ere many minutes had elapsed the peak from foot to summit was in the possession of British soldiers.'

The pursuit pressed on to Lalu, where an enemy counter-attack was repulsed with considerable loss. The next day the tribesmen were attacked again in front of Ambela in the Chamla valley. Seeing themselves in danger of being cut off from their escape route through the Buner Pass, the Akhond's men began to melt away.

The Bunerwals had taken little part in the two days' fighting and now came forward again to keep the agreement previously entered into, to which the Akhond also assented. Accompanied by a few British officers and a small escort of Guides, they completely destroyed the fanatics' base at Malka and undertook to keep them out of their country in future. This undertaking was extremely risky for the officers who had to trust the Bunerwals, but the latter kept their word and ensured the officers' safe return to the column despite the threatening attitude of the fanatics. What had been planned as a three-week operation had taken three months to complete, at a cost of 238 killed and 670 wounded. Nevertheless the tribes between the Indus and the Swat valleys had received a salutary lesson — their casualties were estimated at 3,000 — and the power of the Hindustani fanatics was broken.

In his despatches Chamberlain spoke highly of the Indian soldiers' conduct in this campaign. It was only five years since the

Men of the 93rd Highlanders with prisoners taken at Ambela. Although khaki had been worn during the Indian Mutiny, all the British infantry at Ambela fought in the red serge undress frocks shown here.

end of the Mutiny, and although in those terrible years the Frontier Force regiments had proved loyal, at Ambela many of the sepoys were fighting against their own kith and kin. A soldier of the Guides reported seeing his own father among the enemy and promptly took a shot at him! That there were no desertions and many individual acts of gallantry says much for the British officers who inspired their men's loyalty, but it is also a creditable reflection on the personal honour of those sepoys of the martial races. The campaign also demonstrated that in the more conventional fighting — repulsing a rush with bayonets or assaulting a defended position — British soldiers or Sikhs were the steadiest; they were less adept in the game of stalk and counter-stalk among the high rocks where the Pathans and Gurkhas excelled. At Ambela the tribesmen, when being worsted by their fellow hillmen in uniform, would call out: 'Where are the *lal pagriwalas* (red-turbanned Sikhs) or the *goralog* (Europeans)? They are better sport!'

It was attitudes like this, and the Buner-wals' safe conduct for men they had been fighting only shortly before, that gave Frontier warfare, despite the ferocity, even cruelty with which it was waged by the Pathans, something of the aspect of a sporting contest between two sides who, if not exactly friends, both felt a certain respect and admiration for each other. At Ambela the tribesmen were surprised to discover that their wounded who fell into British hands received medical treatment and were later sent back to their homes. This did not prevent them mutilating and butchering any wounded or prisoners whom they took, but it bred in them a regard for their opponents which they had never felt for their previous oppressors, the Sikh Khalsa of Ranjit Singh.

7

Kabul to Kandahar

If the re-formed Indian Army was now on a sounder footing, it was just as well for in the 1860s, apart from trouble with the Mohmands, Black Mountain tribes and the Orakzais, the armies of the Tsar were on the march again, now that the stresses of the Crimean War were behind them. Whereas formerly the threat had come from the Caucasus and Persia, in the sixties and seventies danger loomed from a new quarter, as Kipling's men of the Mavericks foretold:

Listen in the north, my boys, there's trouble in the wind;
Tramp o' Cossack hooves in front, gray great coats behind,
Trouble on the Frontier of a most amazin' kind,
Trouble on the waters of the Oxus!*

Whether Russia ever seriously meditated an invasion of India in the nineteenth century is now questionable. Certainly she was aware of Britain's sensitivity about the sub-continent, particularly after the upheaval of the Mutiny. By posing a threat there, she hoped to gain advantage in her dealings with Britain elsewhere, notably over the Straits of Constantinople, 'the key to Russia's house', as one Tsar put it. At the time, however, the possibility of a Russian invasion, or at least a Russian-inspired holy war on the borders of and within India, seemed very real to many British politicians, soldiers and officials — and not without reason.

In 1854 some 1,000 miles separated Pesha-

Lord Lytton, Governor-General of India 1876–80, the instigator of the Second Afghan War.

* From the short story 'Mutiny of the Mavericks' in *Life's Handicap.*

Major-General Frederick Roberts VC in Afghanistan 1879 with the six orderlies who accompanied him throughout the campaign: two Punjab Infantry, two 3rd Sikhs and two 5th Gurkhas.

war and Russia's nearest outposts in Central Asia at the northern ends of the Caspian and Aral Seas. Between Cossack and Sepoy there stretched the plain of Turkestan, the desert wastes of the Kara Kum and Kizil Kum, the khanates of Khiva, Bokhara and Khokand, the Hindu Kush and the Pamirs. There were in Russia, as in Britain, the protagonists of both cautious and forward policies, but St Petersburg, like London, found it not always easy to restrain their men in distant places. In the 1860s a circumspect advance began to creep down the line of the Sri-Darya river from the Aral Sea. Prince Gorchakov, the Russian Foreign Secretary and a 'cautious' man, explained in 1864 that this was only a limited advance, but the necessity to subdue disorderly tribes on Russia's frontiers drew her irresistibly further south; he did admit, however, that 'the greatest difficulty is knowing where to stop'. When Tashkent was taken in 1865 and a new province of Turkes-

tan created, its governor, General Kauffmann, seemed not to share this difficulty. By 1868 he had forced a treaty on the Amir of Bokhara, thus obtaining Samarkand and free passage through Bokhara. To the west a base was built at Krasnovodsk on the eastern shores of the Caspian, so that Khiva was now outflanked on both sides. In 1873 it fell, followed three years later by Khokand which became another new Russian province of Fergana. The distance between Russia in Asia and British India had now shrunk to 400 miles. In Fergana its newly-appointed governor, the flamboyant General Skobolev, conceived a plan for a three-pronged invasion of India from Krasnovodsk, Samarkand and Kashgar, supported by the spreading of subversion within the subcontinent.

The implications of these advances had not been lost on British minds in India. Before they had even begun, John Jacob had advocated the occupation of Quetta beyond the Bolan Pass, from which British troops could operate against the flank and rear of an invader making for the Khyber. His recommendation fell on deaf ears until 1876. In 1865 Sir Henry Rawlinson, a member of the Council for India, strongly argued the need for the establishment of a quasi-protectorate over Afghanistan — since the death of Dost Muhammad in 1863 ruled by his son, Sher Ali — so as to permit free movement of British arms to Kandahar and Herat. But the non-intervention school held sway and successive British Governments put their trust in diplomatic negotiations with Russia, with a view to agreeing upon a belt of neutral territory between the Asian possessions of both countries. Nothing very concrete emerged from these except an agreement in 1873 recognising Afghanistan to be within Britain's sphere of influence and Bokhara within Russia's. Meanwhile, Kauffmann's columns continued to advance.

In 1874 a new Conservative Government under Disraeli determined to take a firmer line. The time for a 'forward policy' had come. The Secretary of State for India, Lord Salisbury, discounted fears of a Russian invasion but he was alarmed by the indirect threat of Russian influence, particularly on Afghanistan. He appointed as Governor-General Lord Lytton, a diplomat, a minor poet and son of a novelist, a man with no experience of India but who was much influenced by Sir Henry Rawlinson. Salisbury impressed upon him the necessity for keeping Sher Ali on a tight rein in case the Amir, out of fear for the advancing Russians, 'thinks [it] safer to tie himself to them than to us.'

If brilliant, as some thought, Lytton was also impetuous, seeing only what he wanted to see. It was soon evident, after his arrival, that his vision of the defence of India encompassed British bayonets on the Hindu Kush, perhaps even on the Oxus itself; hold fast there and Skobolev's Mongol vanguards would never reach the vital passes. Such a grand design could only be accomplished by keeping Sher Ali, not on a rein, but in his pocket. His attempts to establish close rela-

Roberts' two Sikh orderlies, Sepoys Dewa Singh and Dehan Singh, 3rd Sikh Infantry, Punjab Frontier Force. Water colour by Colonel Woodthorpe RE.

tions with the Amir being courteously but firmly rebuffed, he became more than ever convinced of the need to pre-empt the Russians in Afghanistan, a conviction that turned to fury when it appeared, in 1878, that he was too late and the opposite had happened.

In 1877 Russia had gone to war with Turkey. The Tsar's troops approached Constantinople, a British fleet sailed to the Dardenelles and Indian troops were sent to Malta. It looked as though Britain and Russia might clash in the Near East. In St Petersburg Skobolev's plan was reconsidered; 15,000 men were on the march between the Oxus and the Hindu Kush. Then, with the Congress of Berlin in mid-1878, the crisis passed and everywhere the Russians pulled back. However, at the very moment the statesmen were beginning to

Group of the 8th (King's) Regiment in garrison at the Peiwar Kotal after its capture in December 1878.

deliberate in Berlin, a Russian mission under General Stolietov arrived uninvited at Kabul. Sher Ali's policy all along had been not to get involved with either Russia or Britain. Now, conscious that he had just refused a British mission, he viewed Stolietov's arrival with dismay but could not forbid him entry. He played for time and was saved any commitment to Russia by St Petersburg's order to Stolietov to withdraw as a result of events in Europe.

Enraged by the Russian's presence in Kabul, Lytton again demanded that Sher Ali receive a British mission. The Amir made no reply and when Neville Chamberlain, its leader, arrived at the mouth of the Khyber in September he was told that any attempt to proceed would be opposed with force. This, Lytton claimed to London, 'deprived the Amir of all further claim on our forbearance', insisting that, if Sher Ali continued to refuse his mission, it must be installed in Kabul by troops. Although Stolietov was preparing to leave Kabul empty-handed, thus removing

any *casus belli* as the Persian withdrawal from Herat had done forty years before, a divided Cabinet in London agreed to give Lytton his head. On 2 November Lytton sent Sher Ali an ultimatum, demanding a favourable reply by the 20th or British troops would cross the border. Now desperate at his plight, the Amir appealed to Kauffmann for military aid, only to be told that the passes through the Hindu Kush were blocked with snow. By then the ultimatum had expired and three columns of British troops advanced into Afghanistan. Sher Ali did not await the outcome. He fled north to plead with the Russians, appointing his son, Yakub Khan, as Regent. The Second Afghan War had begun.

The invasion of Afghanistan followed three lines of advance: in the south from Quetta to Kandahar; in the centre from Kohat through the Kurram Valley, over the Peiwar Kotal, to the Shutargardan Pass, 50 miles from Kabul; in the north from Peshawar through the Khyber to Jalalabad. Sir Donald Stewart's Kandahar Field Force, 12,800 men with 78 guns, had an unopposed march up to Kandahar, which was reached in early January 1879, but the other columns were confronted by Afghan regulars and tribesmen. The latter, particularly the Afridis and Mohmands, continued to attack the lines of communication after the main columns had passed, and a reserve division was fully occupied in dealing with them.

'It was a proud, albeit a most anxious, moment when I assumed command of the Kurram Field Force,' wrote the 46-year-old Frederick Roberts VC. 'Though a local Major-General, I was only a Major in my regiment, and save for a short experience in Lushai, I had never had an opportunity of commanding troops in the field.' His force passed through the pretty Kurram Valley but found its way barred by Afghan regulars entrenched in strong positions with artillery on the pine-covered heights astride the Peiwar Kotal. Since the enemy outnumbered him and their positions entirely commanded the valley floor where he halted, a frontal attack was out of the question. Careful reconnaissance revealed a very rough but possible route up a valley to the right which emerged at the Spingawi Kotal on the extreme left of the Afghan line. Roberts determined to outflank the enemy by a surprise night march up this track with the bulk of his troops, leaving a token force to demonstrate against the Afghan front. After instituting measures to deceive hostile observers as to his intentions, and under great secrecy, he led the flanking column from camp at 10 p.m. on 1 December. With him he had half the 72nd Highlanders, the 5th Gurkhas, the 2nd and 29th Punjab Infantry, the 23rd Pioneers, a mountain battery and four Royal Horse Artillery guns on elephants, 2,263 men in all.

It was bitterly cold as the column toiled upwards, picking its way over huge boulders, wading through icy streams. Secrecy was nearly betrayed when two shots were fired by treacherous Pathan sepoys of the leading battalion, the 29th Punjabis. Time was lost as Roberts changed the order of march, pushing forward the Gurkhas with a com-

pany of Highlanders into the lead. The first light of dawn was breaking as the Gurkhas reached the foot of the Spingawi Kotal where they were spotted. In Roberts' words: 'The Gurkhas rapidly climbed the steep side of the mountain, and swarming into the first entrenchment, quickly cleared it of the enemy; then, guided by the flashes of the Afghan rifles, they pressed on, and, being joined by the leading company of the 72nd, took possession of a second and larger entrenchment 200 yards higher up. Without a pause, the Highlanders and Gurkhas rushed a third position, the most important of all, as it commanded the head of the pass.'

With the Spingawi Kotal won, Roberts pushed on to roll up the enemy line. Heavy fighting ensued and the tangled ground and thick pine forests made control difficult, but by the early afternoon the column was threatening the enemy's rear. The 8th King's

The 72nd Highlanders on parade during the Second Afghan War. This regiment fought throughout the campaign from the Peiwar Kotal to Kandahar. They are uniformed in khaki jackets and red 'Prince Charles Edward Stuart' tartan trews.

Regiment and the 5th Punjab Infantry were now pressing forward from the valley floor up to the Peiwar Kotal. The Afghans, realising that their line of retreat was endangered by Roberts' movement, abandoned their positions and fled, pursued by the 11th Bengal Cavalry which had ridden up the Peiwar track. To have captured such a naturally strong position, defended by eight regular regiments and 18 guns in well-sited entrenchments, was no mean achievement for a numerically inferior force and one undertaken at considerable risk; had the turning movement failed, all would have been lost. As it was the Peiwar Kotal initiated Roberts' reputation as a field commander.

Meanwhile Sir Sam Browne's Peshawar Valley Field Force had entered the Khyber but was held up by the fort of Ali Masjid. This was perched 500 feet up on a hill above the gorge with other fortifications on either side, all held by Afghan regulars with artillery, while tribesmen hovered in the hills on both flanks. Anticipating that he would be obstructed here, Browne had sent one of his three brigades on a wide turning movement through the mountains north of the Khyber to cut in across the enemy rear. A second brigade climbed into the hills to attack the Afghan left while the third advanced frontally. Throughout 21 November the latter, 81st Regiment, 14th Sikhs and 27th Punjabis, endeavoured to storm Ali Masjid but without success, so that at nightfall they were

69

General Sir Sam Browne VC (seated, fourth from left), commander of the Peshawar Valley Field Force, with his staff, 1879.

British infantry of the Peshawar Valley Field Force, 1879.

Camp of the Peshawar Valley Field Force looking towards the heights held by the Afghans either side of Ali Masjid.

pulled back. However during the night the Afghans learned of the turning movement and silently withdrew back up the pass, only to blunder into the 17th Regiment, 1st Sikhs and the Guides lying in wait across their line of retreat. Most were taken prisoner and the way was clear for Browne to advance on Jalalabad.

The three field forces were now established in Afghanistan, although considerable local fighting against tribesmen continued to engage the Kurram and Peshawar columns. When the unfortunate Sher Ali, who never reached Russia, died in February 1879, his son, Yakub Khan, lacking the will and ability to continue the struggle, and further demoralised by British advances to Shutargardan and Gandamak, agreed to negotiate. On 26 May a treaty was signed at Gandamak between Yakub and Major Sir Louis Cavagnari as Lytton's representative. Lytton had conceived little fancy for Yakub as ruler of Afghanistan but his adventure had caused a political row at home, the tribes were in a ferment, cholera was breaking out among the troops and the whole affair was proving extremely costly. Impressed by Yakub's apparent readiness to accede to his demands,

he agreed to recognise him as Amir. Under the treaty the Kurram Valley was ceded to British India, who also gained control of the Khyber Pass and of Afghan foreign policy; to the latter end a mission would be established at Kabul with its safety guaranteed by the Amir. In return Yakub would receive a subsidy of £60,000 and British protection against external aggression. The Peshawar Valley Field Force was withdrawn, its ranks smitten by the cholera. The Kandahar force, also suffering from sickness, would leave as soon as it could, but Roberts' troops would remain in the Kurram.

The latter's first task was to speed Cavagnari on his way as head of the Kabul mission. Cavagnari, of Anglo-French extraction, had had considerable political experience on the Frontier, and had impressed Lytton with his energy, courage and resource. Many shared this opinion and his subordinates found him a rewarding man to work for. On the other hand there were those who found him unpleasantly ambitious and ruthless and, like Lytton, he was inclined to see only what he wanted. Nevertheless, he parted from Roberts in high spirits in July — in marked contrast to the misgivings of the latter who,

Afghan prisoners guarded by sepoys of 45th (Rattray's) Sikhs. This regiment served with the Peshawar Valley Field Force.

convinced of the rebellious and unsettled state of the country, was far from sanguine about the lasting value of the treaty and the mission's chances. Since the Amir had guaranteed its safety, and to avoid antagonizing the Kabulis who had bitter memories of the 1840 occupation, Cavagnari and his assistant Jenkyns were accompanied only by Surgeon Kelly and a small escort of the Guides under Lieutenant Hamilton VC. Everyone knew there were few troops in Asia to match the Guides but the escort numbered no more than 25 sabres and 50 bayonets. If anything were to go wrong, there would be no support nearer than some 60 miles away in the Kurram Valley.

Cavagnari entered Kabul on 24 July, where he was received with due ceremony and installed in the Bala Hissar. At first all seemed serene and if Cavagnari perceived any hostility he did not disclose it in his despatches which exuded calm and optimism. In late August some of the Amir's Kabuli troops were relieved by regiments from Herat. These had played no part in the recent campaign and marched through Kabul with a noisy display of braggadocio and resentment at the presence of the foreign mission. Full of self-esteem they may have been but they were also in arrears over their pay. On 3 September they paraded at the Bala Hissar to be paid, only to find they were given less than they were owed. As they milled about in sullen fury, a cry went up that there was money at the British Residency a few hundred yards away. In a mass they rushed to the Residency where the escort was starting its daily routine. A flurry took place, a shot was fired and the Herati troops rushed off to draw their arms and ammunition.

The Residency was ill-suited for defence, with only a few flat-roofed buildings completely overlooked from several directions and no proper perimeter wall. During the brief respite Hamilton organised the best defence he could, while Cavagnari sent a message to the Amir, claiming his protection.

72

Royal Horse Artillery (left) and 10th Hussars (right) lining the route for the Amir Yakub Khan prior to the signing of the Treaty of Gandamak, 26 May 1879.

Sir Louis Cavagnari with tribal leaders before taking up his post as Resident at Kabul.

British officers of the Guides. Lieutenant Walter Hamilton VC, who defended the Residency at Kabul, stands on the right.

To this and subsequent communications he received no reply, let alone help. Before long the Heratis, now joined by the Kabul mob, returned and the battle began: four Britons and 75 Guides, many of whom were the same race and religion as their assailants, against countless thousands. Cavagnari fell early on, followed by Kelly and Jenkyns, but Hamilton and his brave, loyal Guides still fought desperately, firing from the roof-tops, charging out to bayonet the crews of the guns brought up against them. The buildings were set on fire, the ranks thinned, and eventually Hamilton was killed leading yet another sortie. As the evening sun went down, only a few men remained under a Sikh jemadar of the Guides Cavalry, Jewand Singh. All day the Afghans had called upon the Moslems in the ranks to join them but all such appeals had been rejected with contempt. Now that the British officers were all dead, again the call came, promising quarter. Again it was rejected and Jewand Singh and his few men sallied out to make their last charge. Twelve hours they had fought and 600 Afghan corpses bore witness to their heroic resistance. On the memorial to the defenders of the Kabul Residency at Mardan are inscribed the words: 'The annals of no army and no regiment can show a brighter record of devoted bravery than has been achieved by this small band of Guides.'

News of the tragedy reached India early on 5 September. Immediately the withdrawal from Kandahar was countermanded and Roberts was ordered to advance from the Shutargardan Pass on Kabul with a new force hastily assembled at Kurram. Yakub Khan, faced with a situation which he had neither encouraged nor done anything to prevent, played for safety by appealing for British help at the same time as inciting his troops and people to defend themselves against the impending retribution.

Roberts' newly formed Kabul Field Force, of a cavalry brigade of four regiments, and two infantry brigades, totalling seven battalions, with four batteries, was ready to advance by 27 September. Before he could do so, Yakub Khan rode into his camp with a large escort. Roberts was unimpressed by his appearance — 'a very shifty eye . . . [which]

74

NCOs and sepoys of the Guides Infantry, showing the different types of the 'martial races' that filled its ranks. A photograph taken after the Afghan War, the medal for which is worn by most of the men. The Sikh on the right also wears the Indian Order of Merit, the sepoy's equivalent of the Victoria Cross.

Riflemen of the 4th Gurkhas, part of the Kabul Field Force, December 1879.

Fort Onslow on the Bemaru heights above the Sherpur Cantonment, Kabul, with troops lining the ramparts.

Officers of the 67th Regiment at Kabul, part of the garrison that held the Sherpur Cantonment in the winter of 1879. Note the Sam Browne belts and puttees worn for the first time in this campaign.

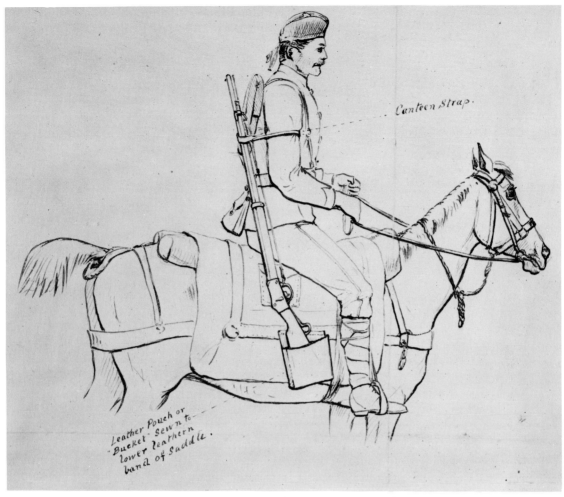

Canteen Strap.

Leather Pouch or Bucket. sewn to lower leathern band of saddle.

A mounted infantryman of the 67th Regiment in Afghanistan. A force of mounted infantry was raised at Kabul in the winter of 1879–80 but the experiment was discontinued after a few months. Drawing by Brigadier-General Baker of the Kabul Field Force.

tallied exactly with the double dealing imputed to him' — and was soon convinced that the Amir, while seeking refuge to save his own skin, was at the same time passing information to his compatriots about the force's strength and plans. Nevertheless he had no choice but to accept the unwelcome guest and begin the advance. So short was he of transport that only one infantry brigade could be moved at a time. Thus, on 5 October, when he reached Charasia, some ten miles from Kabul, and found his way barred by a range of hills cleft by the Logar defile, Macpherson's brigade was a day's march

behind, and he had insufficient troops to seize and hold the hills that evening. He planned to push through the Logar defile next day, but when dawn broke he discovered the route was impassable, the Afghan regulars were in position on the heights, and tribesmen were massing to threaten his camp. Moreover, he learned an Afghan force had got between him and Macpherson. He had only 4,000 men with him and 18 guns, while the enemy numbers were growing steadily. He decided to attack at once.

A cavalry and infantry force, including the 92nd Highlanders, had been sent forward at

British and Indian officers of the 3rd Sikhs, Punjab Frontier Force at Kabul.

first light to reconnoitre the Logar defile, a movement which had induced the Afghans to deploy in great strength on either side of it. Roberts therefore ordered this force to hold the enemy in position there, while Baker's brigade made an outflanking move to the west to assault the more weakly held Afghan right at its extremity. Led by the 72nd Highlanders this brigade fought its way up the very steep slopes against strong resistance from tribesmen and regulars. As the Highlanders gained their first objective, they were reinforced by the 5th Gurkhas and 5th Punjabis and together they battled their way along the ridge towards the heights above the defile. Seeing this threat developing, the Afghan commander transferred troops to his right. This enabled the 92nd to push on up the heights to link up with Baker's men. By the early afternoon, as the dark green kilts of the 92nd mingled with the red tartan trews of the 72nd, the Afghans began to give way

from right to left. When the last defenders were driven from the defile, the 9th Queen's Royal Lancers and the 5th Punjab Cavalry swept through in pursuit.

Riding as ADC to the cavalry brigade commander was Ian Hamilton of the 92nd, who recalled charging with 'the 5th Punjab Cavalry — red puggarees — blue swords flashing . . . Nearer, nearer, every stride nearer! Those dust clouds of the Chardeh valley, flecked here and there with a flicker of moving colour; the foothills speckled with puffs of white smoke . . . Then in the thick of it. Afghans in little knots, or else lying on their backs whirling their big knives to cut off the legs of our horses, a hell of a scrimmage in fact, until the sowars got to work in couples, one with sword uplifted, the other pulling his carbine out of the bucket and making the enemy spring to their feet and be cut down or be shot as they lay. Dust, shouts, shots, clash of steel . . .'

78

The Afghans were routed and on 8 October Roberts entered a silent Kabul accompanied by a chastened Yakub Khan. So chastened that he announced he wished to abdicate, saying that 'he would rather be a grass-cutter in the English camp than the Ruler of Afghanistan.' In due course Lytton had to agree, despite there being no acceptable successor readily available. Until one could be found, the British would have to remain. As Roberts wrote: 'Now I am really King of Kabul. It is not a kingdom I covet and I shall be right glad to get out of it.' The Afghans were told that the Indian Government would consult with the principal chiefs with a view to declaring its intentions 'as to the future permanent arrangements for the good government of the people.' To many of the latter this must have sounded suspiciously like an indefinite foreign occupation.

Meanwhile, there was much to be done.

The ringleaders of the uprising in September were brought to justice and hanged in front of the blackened remains of Cavagnari's Residency. The Bala Hissar was demolished as a symbolic warning. Supplies had to be accumulated against the approach of winter and the partly fortified Sherpur cantonment, a mile north-east of the city, prepared as a habitation for the troops and its defences repaired. It was rectangular in shape, enclosed on the north side by the Bimaru ridge, and on the other three by loop-holed walls, the south and west being high and strong, but the east wall uncompleted and requiring much strengthening; the whole perimeter was four and a half miles long. With no more than 7,000 effectives, of which some 5,500 were infantry — three British (67th, 72nd and 92nd), one Gurkha and five Indian battalions — this gave only one rifle to every $1\frac{1}{2}$ yards, before any were drawn off as a

A party of 72nd Highlanders and Punjab Infantry in ambush at Lataband, the communications post between Kabul and Jalalabad. Water colour sketch by Sergeant Anderson 72nd who appears at left with binoculars. Note the heliograph in the left foreground.

A battery of Royal Artillery at 'Action Front', Afghanistan, 1879.

Men of the 59th Regiment, part of General Sir Donald Stewart's Kandahar Field Force. Lithograph after Lieutenant Irwin, 59th.

19th Bengal Lancers (Fane's Horse) in Afghanistan. This regiment fought under Stewart at Ahmad Khel in April 1880. Water colour.

reserve. With single-shot rifles like the Martini-Henrys and Sniders of the British and Indian infantry, this was a thinly spread firing line against massed, fanatical attacks. However, assisted by his improved defences, which were strengthened by abattis and wire entanglements, and careful siting of his 20 guns, Roberts believed he could hold out if necessary for up to four months.

Trouble broke out in December. Brooding and resentful at their humiliation, Afghans all over the country were fired by their mullahs' call for a jehad against the infidel, and hordes began to converge on Kabul. Rather than await the onslaught Roberts determined to attack and defeat the various columns in detail before they could combine. At first this achieved some success but on 11 December a carefully concerted plan to trap the Afghans west of Kabul foundered due to the cavalry commander, Massy, failing to

stick closely to his orders. His small force of 300 with four guns rode straight into nearly 10,000 Afghans and had to beat a rapid retreat, losing the guns. Heavy fighting continued for the next three days as the infantry strove to dislodge the now combined Afghan forces from the heights south and south-west of Kabul. But with thousands rallying to the enemy standards, and the Kabulis pouring out of the city to join their compatriots, Roberts realised he was hopelessly outnumbered and would have to fall back on Sherpur. Scenting victory, 'the Afghans swarmed down, shouting and brandishing their long knives', wrote Roberts. 'But our brave men were absolutely steady. They took up position after position with perfect coolness; every movement was carried out with as much precision as if they were manoeuvring on an ordinary field day; and the killed and wounded were brought away without the

Indian cavalry in action at the Battle of Maiwand, 27 July 1880. Pen, ink and wash drawing by Macfarlane.

slightest hurry or confusion.' By the evening of 14 December, much to Roberts' relief, his whole force was safely within the walls of Sherpur, as the enemy hordes poured into the city.

Roberts was now virtually cut off from the outside world. The telegraph lines had been cut, cloudy weather interfered with the use of the heliograph, and although a brigade had been ordered forward from Gandamak, it seemed unlikely to arrive. The only reinforcement to reach Sherpur had been the Guides, who had made a forced march through the mountains from the Jagdalak Pass, slipping past the enemy lines around Kabul under cover of darkness. Within the city the mullahs were fanning the flames of fanaticism, already heightened by the festival of Moharram. Then Roberts received information that, on its last day, the 23rd, a beacon would be lit on the Asmai heights by an elderly mullah, Mushk-i-Alam, as a signal for the onslaught on Sherpur.

As the distant cries and throbbing drums wafted across the snow-covered fields on the night of the 22nd, the garrison manned the walls, watching and waiting. All night they stood ready until, just before dawn, the flare from Asmai shot upwards into the dark sky, followed by heavy firing against the east and south walls. As it was still too dark to see, the mountain guns fired star-shells, illuminating the masses coming on across the snow with scaling ladders led by fanatical *ghazis*. The 28th Punjabis and the Guides on the east wall opened fire first, their volleys being quickly taken up by the 67th and 92nd on the south, supported by every gun that could be brought to bear. The Afghans suffered heavily from the disciplined musketry and gunfire, but still they charged fiercely forward to try to place their ladders against the walls. The assault continued unabated until about 10 a.m. when there was a lull, but an hour later they came on again, though with less enthusiasm than before. Roberts was able to send out four guns of G-3 Battery, Royal Artillery, with a cavalry escort to shell the

A Gurkha picquet in khaki summer dress during the Afghan War. Engraving after R. Caton Woodville.

Officers of the 92nd Highlanders, a regiment which took part in Roberts' battles at Kabul and his march to Kandahar.

enemy forming-up positions on the east side from a flank. Gradually the heart went out of the attacks and by 1 p.m. the Afghans were streaming away in flight. The gates were opened and the 9th Lancers, Guides and 5th Punjab Cavalry galloped out in pursuit, scattering the fleeing tribesmen. It was estimated that 100,000 had attacked Sherpur but by next day not a man remained in the sur-rounding hills and villages. This mighty host had been dispersed for the trifling loss of only three killed and 30 wounded.

From 1 January 1880 the country seemed to quieten down but the question of who was to succeed Yakub Khan remained unsolved, and it looked as though Afghanistan would have to be broken up into independent provinces. Herat, untouched by the war so far,

him began with the approval of Lytton, whose views had undergone a complete *volte-face* and who now could not withdraw from Afghanistan quick enough for fear of the continued British occupation provoking the Russians. To the south a governor, or *wali*, was found for Kandahar, which had been re-occupied by Sir Donald Stewart with his division but who now handed over responsibility for its defence to General Primrose of the Bombay Army.

Stewart marched north for Kabul, only to run into strong opposition near Ghazni from a host of Ghilzais and other tribes, incited by the ubiquitous mullah, Mushk-i-Alam. On 19 April they attacked with great ferocity at Ahmad Khel, 3,000 swordsmen coming on at speed in the centre while horsemen on either flank galloped to get round Stewart's hastily formed line. The 59th Regiment was nearly carried away by the onslaught, but with the 3rd Gurkhas and 2nd Sikhs holding firm, and well supported by the artillery and a fine charge by the 2nd Punjab Cavalry, the British battalion rallied. Stewart deployed his reserves and after two hours fierce fighting the Afghans retreated.

Arriving at Kabul in late April Stewart found that not only was he to take over from Roberts — somewhat embarrassingly, though he was the senior — but that Gladstone and the Liberals had come to power in England, and Lytton had resigned. Lytton's enthusiasm for Abdur Rahman had cooled and neither was it shared by Stewart, nor at first by the new Governor-General, Lord Ripon. However, there was increasing support for him in the country, he appeared sensible and friendly enough towards the British, and eventually it was agreed he should be trusted. On 22 July he was proclaimed Amir. Then, six days later, as the British garrison was packing up and preparing to quit Kabul for India, there came shocking news. A brigade of Primrose's Bombay division had been annihilated and the rest were besieged in Kandahar by Ayub Khan of Herat.

The latter had conceived a plan to capture Kandahar and then, having engineered a

was currently governed by Ayub Khan, a brother of Yakub's, but it was now thought that, contrary to former policy, there might be advantage in offering it to the Shah of Persia to wean him away from Russian influence. As for Kabul, the unlikely name of Abdur Rahman, a nephew of Sher Ali's, was put forward; unlikely because for the last twelve years he had been a pensioner of the Russians, following his attempt in 1863 to obtain the throne for his father in preference to Sher Ali. Nevertheless, negotiations with

The 92nd Highlanders at the Battle of Kandahar, 1 September 1880. Painting by Vereker Hamilton, brother of Ian Hamilton of the 92nd.

general uprising against the British, seize the whole country for himself. The lack of any surveillance over Herat had enabled him to make his preparations undetected until the spring of 1880. The Wali of Kandahar had requested British support for his own forces in the area of the Helmand river, but it was not until 4 July, by which time Ayub's army was half-way to the Helmand, that Brigadier-General Burrows was despatched from Kandahar; his force consisted of two Bombay cavalry regiments, an infantry brigade of the 66th Regiment, the 1st and 30th Bombay Infantry, E Battery, B Brigade, Royal Horse Artillery, and a company of sappers. When Burrows reached the Helmand, where the Wali was encamped, the latter's troops absconded, leaving the British 80 miles from their nearest support and with only 2,600 men to counter Ayub, whose 7,500 regular troops and six batteries were being daily swelled by tribesmen along his route as well as the Wali's faithless followers. In order to cover the approaches to Kandahar as best he could, Burrows fell back to Khushk-i-Nakhud, 35 miles to his rear, where he was further ordered to ensure that Ayub did not

bypass Kandahar and make for Ghazni on the road to Kabul, attacking the Afghans if he felt strong enough to do so.

For the next ten days Burrows endeavoured to discover Ayub's line of advance, but his patrolling system, though acquiring some information, was insufficiently thorough to disclose the whereabouts of the main enemy force. On learning that some hostile tribesmen had occupied the village of Maiwand, 13 miles north-east of his position, on 26 July, Burrows decided to expel them and take up a blocking position there. On approaching Maiwand the following day he found to his consternation that Ayub had forestalled him and that he was now confronted by the whole enemy army, between 15–20,000 strong with 30 guns. Though some nearby buildings and a nullah offered a possible defensive position, Burrows formed a line on the open plain to meet Ayub's attack. Hopelessly outnumbered, outgunned and outflanked, his troops stood firm for a while, but his cavalry were reluctant to charge, and the raw young sepoys of the 30th gave way, throwing the hitherto steady 1st Bombay Infantry into confusion. In a panic-stricken mass men of both regiments huddled for protection among the 66th, disordering its line of companies, whose volleys had been holding the enemy at bay. E-B Battery fought their guns nobly until forced to limber up to avoid being overrun, while the 66th, extricating themselves from the shambles, withdrew steadily to the cover of the buildings. Here, as a mob of fugitives fled the field, the British regiment with a few sepoys fought to the end, until the last eleven men left alive charged out to their deaths. Nearly a thousand men were killed, and of the survivors who finally reached Kandahar after a harrowing retreat, only the horse gunners emerged with credit. By the first week in August Ayub Khan was besieging the remainder of Primrose's division in the citadel of Kandahar.

A fortnight after news of the disaster reached Kabul, Roberts marched out with 10,000 men to relieve Kandahar, over 300 miles away. His cavalry brigade included the 9th Lancers and his twelve battalions were evenly divided between three each of British (60th Rifles, 72nd and 92nd Highlanders), Sikh, Gurkha and Punjab infantry. No guns heavier than mule-borne mountain batteries were taken and the baggage was scaled down to the bare minimum. Marching in clouds of dust over mountains and desert in temperatures of up to 110 degrees by day, camping under freezing conditions by night, the column pressed steadily on, cut off from all communications, averaging fifteen miles a day. On 31 August, twenty-one days after he had set out, Roberts marched into Kandahar to find a demoralised garrison. Despite the fatigue of his troops and his own illness, he attacked next day, routing Ayub in a hard-fought, decisive battle outside the city walls.

This epic achievement set the seal on Roberts' reputation as one of the great Victorian military heroes. For his part he never forgot what he owed to the men, British, Indian and Gurkha, whom he had led to victory at the Peiwar Kotal, at Charasia, Kabul and Kandahar. He wrote: 'I looked

The 92nd Highlanders in action at Kandahar. Another version of the battle, by R. Caton Woodville.

The 9th Queen's Royal Lancers in Afghanistan during Roberts' march from Kabul to Kandahar. Water colour by Orlando Norie.

upon them all as my valued friends . . . never had a Commander been better served . . . all were eager to close with the enemy, no matter how great the odds against them.'

With the defeat of Ayub Khan, the policy of fragmenting Afghanistan was abandoned. There was much discussion whether Kandahar should remain under British occupation, but in the end all British garrisons withdrew to India and Abdur Rahman enforced his sovereignty over the whole country. The treaty concluded with him ceded permanently to the Indian Government the strategically important districts of Pishin and Sibi around Quetta, and the Kurram Valley, as well as responsibility for the Afridi country on the Khyber Pass. Although relations with Abdur Rahman would undergo some strain in the years to come, peace between British India and Afghanistan would be preserved throughout his lifetime. Russia was excluded from any hand in his foreign affairs, but her activities beyond the Hindu Kush continued to give concern. The problem of how the North-West Frontier should best be defended remained unresolved and the tribes along it remained as they had always been — resentful of any interference or control.

8

Fixing the Boundaries

The value of Quetta as a military centre and staging post for troops operating on the Kandahar front had been well demonstrated during the war. Its security, and that of the lines of communication forward, was owed to the able work of Robert Sandeman, who had been appointed the Governor-General's Agent for Baluchistan in 1877, following the signing of a treaty which he had skilfully negotiated with the Khan of Kalat and which had resulted in the occupation of Quetta the year before. Sandeman, one of the great Frontier figures, had been commissioned in the Bengal Army in 1856 and, after service with Probyn's Horse in the Mutiny, had transferred to the Punjab Government. His approachability, fair-mindedness and courage in travelling alone and unescorted in tribal territory won him the trust and respect of troublesome and warlike tribes along the common border between the Dera Ghazi Khan district of the Punjab and Sind. His success with these people, and in resolving the differences between the Khan of Kalat and his tribal chiefs, led to his Baluchistan appointment which he held with distinction until his death in 1892. Roberts, who met him when passing through Quetta in 1880, wrote: 'I was greatly impressed by the hold Sandeman had obtained over the country; he was intimately acquainted with every leading man and there was not a village, however out of the way, which he had not visited. 'Sinniman Sahib', as the Natives called him, had gained the confidence of the lawless Baluchis in a very remarkable manner.'

After the Afghan War Sandeman instituted forestry and irrigation schemes, opened up his territory with good communications, organised the collection of land-revenue, and developed the local judicial system based on tribal *jirgas*. He placed the maintenance of order in the hands of local levies and police, with military garrisons held back to reinforce if necessary. With the tribes his watchword was conciliation rather than retribution, in pursuit of which he cultivated and gave every support to tribal leaders who could carry their people with them. Once mutual trust was established, his policies and rulings were obeyed.

Sandeman's methods worked admirably with the Baluchis who by nature tended to be respectful towards authority. However, when Richard Bruce, once his assistant, tried to adopt a similar policy among the Mahsuds of Waziristan when he became Commissioner of the Derajat, he failed due to the anti-authoritarian nature of the Pathans. On the other hand, the Afridis of the Khyber never gave any serious trouble on the Pass for fifteen years when they came under the aegis of Sir Robert Warburton, another administrator of equal, some say greater, stature as Sandeman, who was appointed Political Agent for the Khyber after the Afghan War. Warburton, the son of a Bengal Artillery officer and a niece of Dost Muhammad, also believed in winning the confidence of the tribesmen by a thorough knowledge and understanding of their language and customs. Such was the respect in which he was held that, when he pitched his camp among the Afridi hills, he could write: 'For six or seven weeks my camp was full of men having deadly blood-feuds with one another, armed

Sir Robert Sandeman, the Governor-General's Agent for Baluchistan, 1877–92.

Group of Khyber chiefs and khans with Captain Tucker, who was the Political Officer at Jamrud. A photograph taken after the Afghan War when the Political Agency of the Khyber was established under Sir Robert Warburton.

to the teeth, yet no outrage was ever committed.' His task, however, differed from Sandeman's, in that his aim was control of the pass, rather than control of the tribes; providing the Afridis did not interfere with free movement in the pass, they could do what they liked among themselves.

Elsewhere along the Frontier, in the eighties and early nineties, the old turbulent pattern of raids and ambushes continued until eventually someone somewhere overstepped the mark and another punitive expedition set out. The Black Mountain area, for example, was very unsettled in the eighties, culminating in 1888 in an unprovoked attack on the 5th Gurkhas in which two British officers and four Gurkhas were killed. This small success whetted the appetite of the Black Mountain tribes who gathered to resist the punishment they were warned would be theirs unless they

submitted. A force of five British and ten Indian battalions with four batteries was accordingly despatched. Three columns advanced up parallel spurs on the east side of the mountain, but the chief resistance was encountered by a fourth column whose task was to threaten the crest line from the west. Covered by artillery and Gatling guns, and with its flanks protected by two Indian battalions, the Royal Irish Regiment charged the enemy sangars 'as steadily as if on parade', only to be suddenly counter-charged by fanatical swordsmen pouring out of a ravine. Such surprise onslaughts were a common hazard of Frontier warfare and could prove fatal to inexperienced troops, particularly when caught in the open. On this occasion the Royal Irish kept their heads and calmly shot their assailants down. The enemy positions were abandoned and on the following day the other three columns, who had had a stiff climb but little fighting, reached the crest line.

The expedition remained in the area for another month, destroying villages, reconnoitring, improving communications and generally impressing upon the tribes that, no matter how difficult the terrain, they could not escape retribution for their misdeeds. Resistance was confined mainly to sniping, attacks on small picquets, and, as always in tribal warfare, the rapid follow-up to harass any retirement. At last the tribes which had been in arms decided they had had enough and, once they had made their submissions, the force withdrew, having collected 14,000 rupees in fines, extracted undertakings for future good behaviour, surveyed 177 square miles of uncharted country, and constructed 222 miles of rough roads, at a cost of 86 casualties, of which 25 were killed in action. The tribal undertakings proved durable for a while, but in 1891 a similar sized force had yet again to fight its way into the Black Mountain territory which finally restored peace to this region for the rest of the century.

The early nineties also saw expeditions against the Orakzais of the Miranzai Valley and the Shiranis of the Zhob Valley. The latter proved more a test of endurance and mountaineering than fighting. Its commander, Sir George White, who had won the VC with the 92nd in the Afghan War, dispelled a hostile clan's illusions about the inaccessibility of its territory by demonstrating that a force of Yorkshire Light Infantrymen and Baluch sepoys carrying their arms, ammunition, bedding, rations and water could scale the almost precipitous slopes of a mountain as nimbly as any lightly equipped hillman.

This period witnessed the start of a change in the tactics used by the Pathans. Though excellent marksmen with their *jezails*, they had hitherto favoured the headlong rush of swordsmen to force a decision in a savage hand-to-hand encounter. The morale effect of such a charge, and the speed and surprise with which it was delivered, tested the steadiness of troops to the utmost, particularly when armed with muzzle-loading weapons or even single-shot breech-loaders like the Martini and the Snider. A wild-eyed Ghazi brandishing his *tulwar* could cover a lot of ground in the time it took to reload, and even when hit the impetus of his charge could still carry him forward to hack and slice before he fell. However, from 1888, when the magazine

Afridis of the Khyber, circa 1880. Most of their firearms are still the long-barrelled jezails.

Group of 2nd Battalion Seaforth Highlanders during the Black Mountain Expedition of 1888.

Lee-Metford began to reach British regiments (Indians troops receiving Martinis instead of Sniders), its range and rapidity of fire, particularly when supplemented by Gatlings or Maxim guns, soon impressed the Pathans that the massed charge, certainly in daylight, was not as formidable as once it had been. Likewise, as they too acquired modern rifles, by theft, from gunrunners or by manufacturing copies in their own arsenals, they quickly appreciated the casualties they could inflict at long range without danger to themselves. Edged weapons were not abandoned, and raw or retreating troops would always provide opportunity for a charge, but in general the sniper began to replace the swordsman.

The Pathan's advantage over regular troops lay in his knowledge of his own difficult terrain, over which he could move at great speed, his natural tactical skill and cunning bred of an inbuilt sense of self-preservation, his willingness to wait patiently for a favourable opening, and usually being able to choose when, where and if he would fight. On the other hand, he had little collective discipline and he was highly sensitive to artillery fire, about his line of retreat, and the occupation of any ground higher than that which he occupied. Though on occasions he might attack at night, if the returns were likely to be worthwhile, he was not a natural night-fighter.

The soldier, provided he was well-trained and experienced, had the advantage of discipline and superior firepower, but unless he too was a hillman born, he was less mobile than his adversary. In any case his mobility was that of the regiment or force to which he belonged, which in turn was slowed down by the amount of baggage, ammunition, stores and supplies necessary for its survival in the wilds, and the time and manpower consuming measures essential for its protection, on

95

The Black Mountain Expedition of 1891. Officers and sepoys of the Guides Infantry on the Dilaisi Heights looking down the Indus Valley.

the march and when halted. No column advancing through the mountainous landscape of tribal territory could survive without an advance guard to put up picquets on the high ground to its flanks, and a rear guard to call them down once the column had passed. These could be hazardous operations, particularly when the picquets were ascending and even more when descending, requiring covering fire instantly available. Well-sited and well-conducted picquets in sufficient strength would deter the tribesmen, but the slightest neglect of such precautions, the slightest lack of alertness would invite swift and terrible disaster. Only the most lightly equipped, least encumbered columns could attain any speed through hostile territory. When a column halted for the night, its camp had to be enclosed by a perimeter wall, with an outer ring of picquets posted to give early warning and to prevent snipers from firing

into the camp; all such measures had to be completed, protected all the while, before darkness fell, which further limited the time available for daylight operations. One of the first things troops new to the Frontier had to learn was that the Pathan was above all an opportunist, with a quick and far-seeing eye for the novice or the unwary.

Whatever the merits or otherwise of British political or military action on the Frontier, one thing is certain: it gave the Army in India a valuable experience of active service conditions. A newly-arrived battalion learned more in a week of Frontier operations than in months of manoeuvres at home or in the cantonments of the sub-continent. In the mid-eighties it looked for a while as though this experience would be put to greater test.

Thwarted from establishing her influence in Afghanistan, Russia continued her advance in Turkestan. In command was the

Officers and men, including English infantry and Seaforth Highlanders, in the Indus Valley during the Black Mountain Expedition of 1891.

expansionist Skobolev, who had earlier begun the construction of a strategic railway eastwards from Krasnovodsk on the Caspian. His views on how to further Russia's aims in the Balkans and Near East by threatening Britain in India were as strongly held as ever. In January 1881 7,000 Russian troops with 60 guns captured the Turcoman fortress of Geok-Tepe on the border of northern Persia which stood in the path of Skobolev's railway. Surprised and encouraged by the British evacuation of Afghanistan, the Russians occupied Merv, only 130 miles from the Afghan border, in 1884, an act which so alarmed the British Government that it was accused of 'Mervousness'. With Tsarist forces now so close to a border which was ill-defined, and mindful of its obligations to assist Abdur Rahman against external aggression, Britain suggested that a joint Russo-British commission should settle a frontier

line acceptable to both and to Afghanistan. This was agreed but took some time to set up. Meanwhile, the Russian generals on the spot continued to edge forwards to Pandjeh, the last oasis before the Afghan frontier and only 30 miles from it. Abdur Rahman sent troops to defend it and as the situation on his border intensified, so did the diplomatic exchanges between London and St Petersburg. In March 1885 the British Ambassador warned the Russian Foreign Secretary against attacking Pandjeh, and that any subsequent move in the direction of Herat would be tantamount to war between Britain and Russia. He was given soft words of denial that any such intentions existed but while the diplomats talked, the soldiers acted. On 30 March General Komarov attacked and routed an Afghan force before Pandjeh and occupied it. The place was no more than a small caravanserai with a water-hole stuck in the middle of a desert, but in the spring of 1885 it suddenly became the focus of international attention, as the great Powers of Europe waited to see how Britain would react; if Britain and Russia went to war in Central Asia, the balance of power in Europe would almost inevitably be upset. In London Gladstone and the Liberals were in office but even they were not prepared to ignore the challenge thrown down by Komarov. Gladstone asked the Commons for a war credit and orders were telegraphed to India for the mobilisation of two army corps. Abdur Rahman, who happened to be in India on a state visit at the time, was assured by the Governor-General of Britain's support should Russia invade his country, and in token of British sincerity engineers were sent from India to improve Herat's defences, while a consignment of rifles and guns passed through the Khyber for the Afghan Army.

For a few weeks the threat of war hovered, but as soon as it was clear that Britain meant business, Russia backed down and diplomatic negotiations were resumed to settle the general line of the Russo-Afghan frontier. The detailed work of delimiting it on the ground was carried out by the joint Boundary Commission, any major differences of opinion being referred back to the respective governments. In 1887 the border was finally agreed, not without difficulty, but the further extension of Skobolev's railway to Merv, Bokhara and eventually Tashkent, and the concentrations of Russian troops in those regions continued to cause concern in India.

The 1885 scare led Roberts, who shortly after was appointed Commander-in-Chief India, to reconsider the defence of the North-West Frontier, finding himself in disagreement with an earlier committee's report which had recommended the construction of numerous fortifications along the border. He maintained that lines of communication were of 'infinitely greater importance, as affording the means of bringing all the strategical points on the frontier into direct communication with the railway system of India and enabling us to mass our troops rapidly.' Furthermore such communications would

improve relations with the frontier tribes, whose hostility could greatly imperil any offensive or defensive troop movements, for 'there are no better civilizers than roads and railways.' He regarded attempts to fortify every entry point through the passes as a waste of money, but that strongholds for the protection of depots and as firm bases, either for attack or defence, were necessary on the main routes into India from Kandahar and Kabul. For the first he selected a position in the rear of the Kwaja-Amran range which would protect Quetta and the Bolan Pass. As to the second, the committee had urged the building of entrenchments at the mouth of the Khyber and a large magazine at Peshawar, but Roberts thought this far too far forward in view of its vulnerability to outflanking and possible tribal disturbances in the Peshawar Valley. Instead he chose a location close to Attock, on the south bank of the Kabul river and commanding the passage of the Indus, to which the garrisons of Peshawar and Nowshera could fall back and await reinforcements. The other passes, he felt, merely required a careful study of the ground with a view to determining the best course of action therein, should any become necessary.

By the time Roberts gave up command of the Army in India in 1893, he had achieved, he said, 'the supreme satisfaction of knowing that I left our North-West Frontier secure, so far as it was possible to make it so, hampered as we were by want of money. The necessary fortifications had been completed, schemes for the defence of the various less important positions had been prepared, and the roads and railways, in my estimation of such vast importance, had either been finished or were well advanced.'

Vital though the railways may have seemed to Roberts, to Abdur Rahman they appeared a threat, particularly that pushed forward, 'like a knife into my vitals', through Quetta to Chaman, only 50 miles east of Kandahar. Though he had welcomed British support in the Pandjeh crisis, he was less than happy about other aspects of the 'forward policy': the control of the Khyber and

Commanders, 1885. From left: General Hon A. E. Hardinge, C-in-C Bombay; General Sir Frederick Roberts, C-in-C Madras; General Sir Donald Stewart, C-in-C India, whom Roberts succeeded in that appointment.

the Kurram Valley, the expeditions against tribes of his own race and religion. Increasingly, he felt that the British were nibbling away at his territory and in 1892 he warned the Governor-General, Lord Lansdowne: 'If you should cut [the frontier tribes] out of my dominions, they will neither be any use to you nor to me. You will always be engaged in fighting or other trouble with them, and they will always go on plundering. In your cutting away from me these tribes, you will injure my prestige in the eyes of my subjects, and will make me weak, and my weakness is injurious for your government.' Not content with such warnings he used his influence among the Frontier Pathans to spur them into action which would demonstrate the validity of his comments.

Then, unexpectedly, his truculent mood turned into one of co-operation, and he

agreed that a mission under Sir Mortimer Durand, Lansdowne's Foreign Secretary, should come to Kabul to discuss the delimitation of the Indo-Afghan border. Even more surprising was the amount of territory the Amir was prepared to yield, seemingly without demur. It has been said that his agreement was secured under duress, that he was bribed by an increase to his subsidy, or that he was too proud to admit he did not understand Durand's careful explanations of lines drawn on maps with which he may not have been familiar. Whatever the case, he signed a formal agreement in November 1893 and henceforth the political boundary between India and Afghanistan, known then and since as the Durand Line, enclosed within British territory the lands of Chitral, Bajaur, Swat, Buner, Dir, the Khyber, Kurram and Waziristan. Over the next two years a Commission demarcated the line on the ground by a series of pillars.

Such markings meant little to the tribesmen, but their purpose was to define responsibility for tribal disorders on either side of the line, across which neither the Amir nor the Indian Government was to interfere. It has been criticised by Sir Kerr Fraser-Tytler, the historian of Afghanistan, as 'illogical from the point of view of ethnography, of strategy, of geography'. It divided the Pathans, even cutting the territory of the Mohmands in two, it greatly increased the responsibilities of the Indian Government, and it heightened the chances of conflict with the tribes and, when he appreciated what he had given away, with the Amir. Despite evidence of Afghan influence subverting the tribes on the British side in following years, the Durand Line continued to be observed as the political boundary between Afghanistan and India.

With its demarcation, British India now had two borders on the Frontier. First there was the old, administrative border, largely outside tribal territory and inherited from the Sikhs, up to which the Punjab Government ruled, policed, taxed and dispensed justice as occurred in the rest of India, through the Commissionerships of Peshawar, embracing the northern districts of Hazara, Peshawar and Kohat, and of the Derajat, which included the southern districts of Bannu, Dera Ismail Khan and Dera Ghazi Khan. Beyond and up to the political border with Afghanistan was the tribal territory in which only influence was exercised, through a system of political agencies, like that established for the Khyber after the Afghan War. Kurram, also ceded after that war, became an agency in 1892, and was followed by those of the Tochi Valley and Wana or, as they were described, North and South Waziristan. The agents in each were responsible to the Punjab Government. A fifth agency was added later, as will shortly be seen.

In the years that followed the demarcation of the Durand Line, and stemming directly or indirectly from it, the Frontier was to experience tribal warfare on a scale never seen before. Before passing on to that, some

reorganisation of the army that fought it must be noted. After the Second Afghan War a number of regiments were disbanded, chiefly from the Madras Army. The anomalous position of the Punjab Frontier Force being outside the control of the Commander-in-Chief India was rectified in 1886 and the Frontier Force became part of the Bengal Army, though retaining its special character, traditions and privileges. This was followed by measures designed to achieve greater unification of the three separate armies of Bengal, Madras and Bombay. As a first step the

Types of the Punjab Frontier Force, circa 1887. From left: Sepoy and sowar of the Guides; Jemadar, 1st Punjab Infantry; Sowar, 1st Punjab Cavalry; Sepoy 3rd Sikh Infantry; Gunner, No. 1 Kohat Mountain Battery; Rissaldar, 3rd Punjab Cavalry. Chromolithograph after R. Simkin.

practice of commissioning British officers for Indian regiments into separate pools of officers known as 'staff corps' for each Army was abolished in 1891 in favour of one Indian Staff Corps. In 1895 the Presidency Armies were replaced by one Army in India (including British regiments) divided into four Commands: the Punjab, Bengal, Madras and Bombay, the latter taking in Sind and Baluchistan. The upper reaches of the Fron-tier came therefore under the Punjab Command, the lower under Bombay. The regiments retained their numerals and old Presidency titles — Bengal Infantry, Bombay Cavalry — from which the somewhat pejora-tive 'Native' had been dropped in 1885. Each Command came under a lieutenant-general responsible to the Commander-in-Chief. India, the old individual commanders-in-chief being abolished.

Sepoy of the 3rd Sikhs, Punjab Frontier Force, 1887. He wears the Indian General Service Medal 1854–95, the Second Afghan War Medal and the Kabul-Kandahar Star. The photograph on which the central figure of the previous illustration was based.

Apart from Frontier operations, the prime task of the Army was held to be internal security — the memory of the Mutiny died hard — so the regiments, British and Indian, cavalry and infantry, were not grouped into brigades or divisions but spread about in small garrisons all over the sub-continent. Complementing this type of deployment were three other measures designed to insure against any possible repetition of 1857: the proportion of British troops to Indian was raised from about one in nine before the Mutiny to one in three; all artillery was concentrated in British, *i.e.* the Royal Artillery, hands, except for the mountain batteries; and the personal weapons of Indian troops were always to be inferior to those of British.

This system may have held down India satisfactorily but it was inefficient for war, either on the Frontier or elsewhere. The regiments within Commands continued to be localised as in the Presidency Armies with consequent variations in readiness and efficiency: a regiment in the Punjab Command obviously needed to be more on its toes than one in Madras. If some emergency required the sudden assembly of a field force, the brigades for it were made up with regiments earmarked for the purpose, each brigade usually having one British with three or four Indian or Gurkha battalions, or two and two. However the regiments picked did not necessarily know the senior officer under whose command they were placed, nor he them, and neither might they have trained with the other regiments with whom they were brigaded. Thus a brigade or division plunged into a Frontier war would have to take the field as an untried formation, commanders, staffs and troops having to get to know each other as they went along. Given the Pathans' natural aptitude for war and their perception in spotting any weakness, this was far from an ideal arrangement.

9

This Awful Fort

It could be said that the 1890s witnessed the high noon of the British Empire. It was a decade when the British people were first truly seized by the might of their Empire, when their enthusiasm and interest were fired by the distant deeds of the administrators, soldiers and sailors who held it, resulting in a frenzy of patriotic and imperial fervour which culminated in the Diamond Jubilee of 1897. Two years before, in a remote and distant corner of that Empire, there had occurred an incident whose archetypal ingredients — a beleaguered garrison with columns hastening to its relief — had filled the newspapers, bringing drama, suspense and a sense of identification with the fate of gallant men to countless Victorian breakfast tables.

In the far north of British India, below where the eastern peaks of the Hindu Kush merge into the Pamirs, lay a sparsely populated region of snow-capped mountains and precipitous valleys of which the chief centres were, from east to west, Hunza and Nagir, Gilgit and Chitral. This area had been under the nominal control of the Maharajah of Kashmir, who was responsible for its security to the Punjab Government, but in 1877 it came under the Foreign Department of the Indian Government. A British agency was established at Gilgit but was closed in 1881. In the late eighties it was re-opened due to increasing lawlessness in Hunza-Nagir and, more disturbing still, reports of growing Russian activity in the Pamirs; small Cossack patrols had even appeared in Hunza and Chitral. At the same time British officers were despatched to improve the Kashmir State Forces.

In 1891 the agent, Colonel Algernon Durand, decided to construct a road through Hunza-Nagir, giving prior notice of his design. The ruler of Hunza, who claimed direct descent from Alexander the Great, sent a most uncompromising reply, threatening to cut off Durand's head! The agent therefore advanced with a small force of two companies of the 5th Gurkhas and three battalions of Kashmir infantry, but found his march opposed at the fortress of Nilt. In the little campaign that followed — sometimes called the War on the Roof of the World — three officers won the Victoria Cross.* After the success of this expedition no further trouble occurred in this region until, four years later, Chitral burst into flames.

A little larger than Wales, Chitral was locked in on all sides by mountains, towering peaks that never lost their snows, a wild and desolate terrain only softened by the occasional small fertile valley where willows lined the streams, almond trees blossomed in spring and the plane trees turned copper in the autumn. Its remote inaccessibility had left it undisturbed since the British had first arrived on the North-West Frontier; but its strategic location between the Punjab to the south, and Afghanistan, both to the west and north, where only the narrow Wakhan panhandle intervened between the Russians in the Pamirs, gave it an importance that could not be overlooked. This was heightened after 1893 when it became incorporated

* Captain Aylmer, Royal Engineers; Lieutenant Boisragon, 5th Gurkhas; Lieutenant Manners–Smith, Indian Staff Corps.

Chitral Fort with the Kunar river in the foreground.

in British territory, and a power vacuum ensued following the death of its ruler or Mehtar, Aman-ul-Mulk, who had earned the enmity of his subjects by his tyrannical reign of thirty years.

The Chitralis were a non-Pathan people of some superficial charm which cloaked an endless capacity for greed, cruelty and treachery — characteristics displayed to the full when the Mehtar died in 1892. His second son, Afzul-ul-Mulk, having murdered three of his step-brothers and a few inconvenient notables, proclaimed himself Mehtar, only to be slain in his turn by his uncle, Sher Afzul who seized power, probably with the covert backing of the Afghan Amir, who for some time was thought to have designs on Chitral. Sher Afzul's perfidy availed him nothing, for when the rightful but reluctant heir, Aman's eldest son Nizam, who had been living at Gilgit, was emboldened by British support to press his claim, Sher

Afzul's support melted away and he fled to Kabul. Nizam was installed as Mehtar in December 1892 under the supervisory eye of Surgeon-Major Robertson, lately of the Indian Medical Service but soon to be appointed Political Agent at Gilgit. This done, Robertson returned to Gilgit, leaving his assistant, Lieutenant Gurdon, at Chitral to keep an eye on things. For a while all was quiet though Nizam, feckless, drunken and with growing distaste for the job, proved neither popular nor efficient. Then, in January 1895, he too was murdered by his apparently half-witted and harmless step-brother, Amir-ul-Mulk.

Amir's treachery was part of a conspiracy plotted by Sher Afzul to regain Chitral for himself, aided and abetted by a powerful Pathan chief, Umra Khan of Jandol, who had made himself master of all Dir and Bajaur, and was not averse to adding Chitral to his domains. Though nominally united,

104

each of the three was more than ready to betray his co-plotters if thereby he could gain advantage for himself, while in the background the Afghans watched closely to gain whatever profit they could reap. Gurdon, alone at Chitral with only eight Sikhs as escort, was in a suddenly perilous situation but calmly refused to recognise Amir-ul-Mulk as Mehtar until he had received instructions from Robertson.

Though the route between Gilgit and Chitral was at its worst, Robertson set out at once with a small body of troops and, after a very difficult march, reached Gurdon at the end of the month. Soon he learned that both Umra Khan and Sher Afzul were not far off with large bodies of followers and that the latter was demanding the British should leave Chitral. Unmoved by threats and conscious that to withdraw would invite disaster,

Robertson deposed Amir-ul-Mulk, replaced him by his ten-year-old brother, Shuja, and concentrated his force in Chitral fort. On 3 March news was received that Sher Afzul was approaching with a large force. Captain Campbell, the senior military officer, led out a reconnaissance but was ambushed by some 1,200 tribesmen. Campbell was badly wounded, another British officer was killed and 56 sepoys were casualties. Any Chitralis who had been wavering in their allegiance promptly went over to the enemy, and Robertson and his men found themselves surrounded and cut off from the outside world.

The fort they occupied was on the right bank of the Chitral or Kunar river, some 45 yards from the water's edge. It was 80 yards square with 25-feet-high walls of masonry held together by a cradlework of wooden beams. At each corner was a tower, while on the north face alongside the river was a fifth tower overlooking a covered way leading out to the water. Since the fort was dominated by high ground, some rearwards protection for men manning the parapets had to be improvised. Though Robertson was in overall charge, actual command of the troops now devolved on Captain Townshend of the Central India Horse; these consisted of 300 Kashmir Infantry, of doubtful quality except for a leavening of Gurkhas, and the hardcore of the defence, 99 rifles of the 14th Sikhs under Lieutenant Harley. The only other British officers were Gurdon and Surgeon-Captain Whitchurch. Taking refuge in the fort were 52 Chitralis, among them the little Mehtar, Shuja, with members of his household and some women, and 57 other non-combatants. There was sufficient ammunition to give the Sikhs' Martinis 300 rounds a rifle and 280 for the Kashmiris' Sniders.

The besiegers, Sher Afzul's Chitralis, at first confined themselves to sniping into the fort but, on the night of 7/8 March, having been joined by some thousand of Umra Khan's Pathans, they made the first of what would be several attempts to cut off the fort's water supply. A heavy fire was opened on the

The defenders of Chitral, 1895. Surgeon-Major Robertson (sitting) and, from left, Lieutenant Harley, 14th Sikhs; Lieutenant Gurdon, Political Officer; Captain Townshend, Central India Horse.

The deposed Mehtar of Chitral, Amir-ul-Mulk, guarded by Sikhs with a Kashmir sepoy in the right foreground.

Chitral Fort from the inside looking out over the Kunar river.

north-west face to distract the defenders, while another party set fire to the watchtower guarding the waterway. The flames were doused by water-carriers detailed off for this purpose while volleys from the walls drove off the attackers. The covered way to the river remained intact, but the need to preserve this vital artery and the ever-present danger of fire, so much of the fort's structure being of wood, continued to be a major preoccupation of the defence.

Robertson was confident that the messages he had got out before the siege began would bring relief, but the first news he received from the outside world brought him no comfort. A convoy of ammunition and engineering stores under Lieutenants Edwardes and Fowler had set out for Chitral on 5 March from the small garrison at Mastuj on the Gilgit road. The following day Edwardes learned for the first time that Chitral was under siege and that his march would be opposed. He pushed on to the village of Reshun where he was attacked by a large force under Muhammad Isa, a foster brother of Sher Afzul's. Here, barricaded in a huddle of squalid, flat-roofed dwellings he held out until the 13th when, during a truce called by the enemy, he and Fowler were treacherously seized. They fully expected to be killed, but were held as hostages, eventually being moved after a terrible journey to Umra Khan's fort at Kila Drosh, south of Chitral. Nor was this all, for on 11 March Captain Ross and his company of the 14th Sikhs were ambushed in a defile while marching to Edwardes' aid, from which only his sub-altern, Jones, and fourteen sepoys, most of them badly wounded, managed to reach safety. Some of Ross' Sikhs who were captured were butchered in cold blood by the Chitralis, and many rifles and much ammunition fell into enemy hands as a result of these two actions.

The Chitralis were quick to inform Robertson of the setbacks, hoping the news would demoralise the garrison which, despite the possibility of treachery from the Chitralis within the walls and the unreliability of the Kashmir Infantry, was still resisting every attack successfully. The need for continual vigilance by day and night, both within and outside the fort, placed an increasing strain on the British officers. Furthermore some 60 rifles were now unserviceable and by the end of March provisions were running short, the officers being reduced to eating horseflesh. Three days heavy rain followed by a snap of cold weather made life uncomfortable, while the poor sanitation and crowded conditions bred dysentery and an appalling stink throughout the confines of the fort, but, though ill himself, Robertson's resolution and that of his companions never faltered. While Townshend ran the defence, Robertson devised schemes to outwit and spread dissension among the besiegers. He was constantly worried about the fate of Edwardes and Fowler and whether help was on the way, until one day, after nearly a month's siege, while parleying over the former, he learned encouraging news of the latter.

When news of Umra Khan's invasion of Chitral reached the Indian Government, he was sent an ultimatum to withdraw by 1 April. At the same time a division of troops under Major-General Sir Robert Low began to mobilise at Peshawar, prior to concentrating at Nowshera for a possible advance from the south: a distance of some 160 miles across two river obstacles, through the largely unknown country of Swat, Dir and Bajaur, until the 10,000 feet high Lowarai Pass was reached at the southern boundary of Chitral state. Before Low was ready to move, a much smaller force consisting of a half-battalion (400 men) of the 32nd Punjab Pioneers under Colonel Kelly, with two guns of the Kashmir Mountain Battery, set out from Gilgit on 23 March to cover the 220 miles of very poor road to Chitral.

Marching without tents and with the bare minimum of baggage carried by coolies, Kelly covered the first hundred miles by the 31st but was then faced by the formidable Shandur Pass, 12,000 feet high, some ten miles long and deep in snow. Since it was clear that the gun mules would never negotiate the snow with their loads, it looked as though the guns would have to be left behind, until the sepoys volunteered to manhandle them forward. The task was frightful. In addition to heaving the guns through the snow, in places three to five feet deep, each man was burdened with his rifle, ammunition, rations, greatcoat and poshteen. By day the men poured with sweat from their exertions under the sun, while its glare affected many with snow-blindness. At night the thermometer dropped below zero, causing the men, mostly Sikhs from the hot Punjab, to suffer dreadfully from frostbite and exposure due to the lack of any shelter. Nevertheless, it was finally accomplished and by 5 April the foot of the pass was reached. Four days later the advance was halted by 400 tribesmen in a strong position blocking the track. Though he had only half his force in hand, Kelly at once opened fire with the mountain guns and within an hour his Pioneers had driven the

enemy from their sangars. The way was now clear to link up with the small garrison of Kashmir Infantry holding the fort of Mastuj, where a halt of three days was made to reorganise the column for the final 50 miles to Chitral, where Robertson was still holding out despite continued attacks.

While Kelly's men were struggling across the Shandur Pass, Low's division, of three infantry brigades plus divisional cavalry, artillery and engineers, having left Nowshera on 1 April, was fighting its way into Swat where the tribes were out. There were three possible entry points: the Malakand, Shakot and Morah passes, each about 3,500 feet high and some seven miles apart. Feinting against the two latter, Low launched his 2nd Brigade against the Malakand with the 1st Brigade in support. The tribesmen were in strength along the heights either side of the crest of the pass, while more occupied a series

Colonel Kelly (with beard) with British and Indian officers of the 32nd Punjab Pioneers who marched from Gilgit to relieve Chitral.

1st Battalion King's Royal Rifle Corps parading before departure on the Chitral Relief expedition as part of General Low's division.

of sangars dotting the spurs leading down from the main position. The Guides Infantry and the 4th Sikhs scaled two very steep spurs to turn the enemy right flank, as the 2nd King's Own Scottish Borderers and 1st Gordon Highlanders attacked frontally covered by the guns. The difficult nature of the ground slowed up the flanking movement, but the 1st King's Royal Rifle Corps and 15th Sikhs of the 1st Brigade then pushed their way up a watercourse between the Borderers and the Guides to lend weight to the attack. As each sangar was cleared, the assaulting infantry came under fire from another behind, to which was added the hazard of huge boulders being rolled down the steep slopes from the heights above. On the right the 1st Bedfords and 37th Dogras of the 1st Brigade managed to turn the enemy's left, pursuing the retreating tribesmen to the Swat river as the other battalions carried the crest of the pass with a bayonet charge after five hours fighting. Enemy casualties were calculated at between 1,200 and 1,500, but Low lost only seventy in killed and wounded.

Private Pridmore of the Bedfords believed this to be because, 'the Swat races are very poor marksmen. Their usual method is to sight their weapons for a certain mark beforehand, and they keep firing at this throughout the battle. If any of our men got within the line of fire they would probably be hit, but our method was first to send a few men forward to make a dust and induce the enemy to fire. Then we noticed where the bullets hit, kept just outside the mark, and picked off our opponents.'

On the following day, 4 April, the 1st Brigade was concentrated in the lush Swat valley while the divisional baggage train — some 30,000 pack animals — was moved over the Malakand. The brigade was threatened all day by a mass of tribesmen hovering in the surrounding hills, and towards evening some 2,000 of them poured down on to the plain, making for a rocky outcrop held by the 37th Dogras. Out of sight behind the Dogras was a squadron of the Guides Cavalry under Captain Adams. As the enemy came racing across the flat open

Group of 2nd Battalion King's Own Scottish Borderers, part of General Low's relief force for Chitral.

View towards the Malakand Pass, stormed by General Low's division on 3 April 1895.

ground, this squadron broke from cover and charged. Though they only mustered 50 sabres, their sudden, dramatic onslaught checked the Swatis who had never faced cavalry before; horrified by the galloping horses and the flashing sabres, the tribesmen broke and fled to the safety of the hills. The historian of the Guides, Colonel Younghusband, commented: 'The execution done was considerable, but greater still was the moral effect. From that day forth a mounted man was a power in the land.'

Closing up to the Swat river, the leading troops found the crossing opposed by about 4,500 tribesmen. While the mountain guns and infantry opened a long-range fire from in front, the Guides Cavalry and 11th Bengal Lancers crossed the river higher up and came down on the enemy from a flank, enabling the infantry to wade across unopposed and occupy the fort of Chakdara to protect the building of a bridge. In the meantime cavalry patrols pushed forward to the next obstacle,

the Panjkora river, 25 miles ahead.

If 4 April had been the day of the Guides Cavalry, then the 13th was surely that of their infantry comrades. The Panjkora was flooded but on the night of the 12th/13th the Guides Infantry got across a footbridge constructed the day before, with the task at daybreak of clearing the hills in front which commanded the crossing place, so that the main body could cross in safety. Later that night the bridge was washed away so that by dawn the Guides were isolated on the far bank. Unwilling to remain inactive, Colonel Fred Battye in command left two companies to hold the bridgehead and led out five more to sweep the high ground and burn some hostile villages. All went well until about 9 a.m. when some 5,000 enemy were seen massing on his right flank, obviously with the intention of cutting the Guides off from the river. Battye reported the situation by heliograph to Low, who ordered him to retire.

What followed is vividly described by

Prisoners guarded by sepoys after the taking of the Malakand Pass.

Younghusband: 'Before the anxious eyes of an army, so near yet so powerless to help, the Guides commenced their retirement. With the great mountains as an amphitheatre the drama began to unfold itself before the gaze of waiting thousands. Only the strongest glasses could make out the position of the Guides; but apparent to the naked eye of all was the great straggling mass which was falling with relentless swiftness on the narrow neck of the communications with the bridge. With cool intrepid courage, with a deliberation which appeared almost exasperating to the onlookers, Colonel Battye and his men took up the challenge. Little parties of soldiers could be descried slowly sauntering back a few yards only, then disappearing among the rocks with a rattle of rifle-fire. Then back came more little parties of soldiers, all seemingly sauntering, all with the long sunny day before them. And after them bounded great waves of men in blue and men in white, only to break and stagger back before those little clumps of rock in which the

Types of the Guides Infantry. From left: sepoy, Indian officer (full dress), lance-naik and havildar.

112

Maxim gun detachment of 1st Battalion Devonshire Regiment during the Chitral campaign. These were the guns that covered the withdrawal of the Guides over the Panjkora river.

rearmost soldiers lay. "Get back, get back!" shouted the spectators on the eastern bank in impotent excitement. But no word of this reached the Guides on the slopes; nor would they have heeded had they heard, for they had been born and bred to the two simple maxims, "Be fiery quick in attack, but deadly slow in retirement". And so slowly back they came, and in their wake lay strewn the white and blue figures, all huddled up or stark and flat.'

As the Guides companies fought their way down the last spur, each covering the other, part of the enemy moved to cut them off from the bridgehead on the flat open ground between the foot of the spur and the river. Seeing this, the two companies which had been left behind advanced to check the movement. At the same time the mountain guns and the Maxim detachment of the 1st Devons opened fire as soon as the enemy came within range, while the whole 2nd Brigade lined the east bank to give support

with their rifles. Despite this flanking fire, the enemy pressed hotly forward to close quarters as the Guides fell back across the barley fields. Here, just before safety was reached, Fred Battye was mortally wounded, the third of a famous Guides family to fall in action. Covered by the rest of the force, the Guides reached their bridgehead, but the enemy continued to threaten everywhere with great daring until after darkness fell. In this classic example of Frontier warfare, the Guides admirably demonstrated the importance of deliberation and steadiness in withdrawal.

A suspension bridge was constructed over the Panjkora, during which time Major Deane, Low's Political Officer, began negotiations with Umra Khan which successfully obtained the release of Lieutenants Edwardes and Fowler. On 17 April the 3rd Brigade had a skirmish near Umra Khan's fort at Munda but the latter's followers melted away to the west. However, Chitral was still 85 miles away and Low now received news that the garrison, though still holding out, was at its last gasp. He therefore ordered Brigadier-General Gatacre, with a small, lightly-equipped force of the 1st Buffs, a company of the 4th Gurkhas and the Derajat Mountain Battery, to press on at best speed across the high Lowarai Pass.

On the same day as the Guides' fight on the Panjkora, Kelly's little force was once again in action far to the north. While reorganizing at Mastuj, Kelly reconnoitred forward to find that a body of 1,500 Chitralis under Muhammad Isa had taken up a strong position astride a valley at Nisa Gol. The road followed the line of a river which flowed close under some precipitous cliffs on its south bank. On the north side a stretch of open ground lay between the river and the mountains bordering the valley. From these mountains a ravine between 200–300 feet deep with perpendicular sides ran right across the open ground back to the river. The only way across had been demolished by the Chitralis, who had also built strong sangars of timber and rock along the ravine, as well as on the high ground to left and right. With his force now increased by 200 Kashmir Infantry and Hunza levies, Kelly advanced against this formidable position on 13 April.

The mountain guns opened fire at 500 yards range against the sangars on the enemy left, whose fire commanded the frontal approaches. The gunfire drove the Chitralis into open ground, where they were cut down by volleys from Kelly's main body, enabling the levies to scale the hills so as to reach positions from which they could threaten the enemy rear. The guns and the Pioneers then turned their fire on the enemy centre while other riflemen engaged the sangars across the river. Three officers and twelve Kashmiri sappers went forward to try to find a way across the ravine. With the aid of ropes and ladders they descended into the depths and luckily found a goat track on the far side which could be climbed on all fours. Emerging cautiously on the enemy side, they were thankful to see that a Pioneer company was in position behind them ready to give covering fire but, as they beckoned the Pioneers to

follow, a slab of gun-cotton which had been left on the home bank was struck by a chance bullet and began to fizz. To avoid the explosion the Pioneers fell back and the Chitralis, having begun to slip away, surged back to their sangars, on which a heavy fire was resumed. However, the levies' attack round the enemy left now developed and, as the Pioneers came forward again to cross the ravine, the Chitralis streamed away before they could be cut off.

Nisa Gol had long been considered an impregnable position in Chitral and its loss adversely affected the tribes' will to continue fighting. Kelly, on the other hand, was unaware of this and knew that between him and Chitral, still a week's march away, lay the dangerous defiles where Edwardes and Ross had been ambushed over a month before. Though he had no news of the besieged garrison, he appreciated that if Robertson was still secure he must be reached soon, and accordingly advanced on a safer, though far more difficult route through the hills, rather than risk his small force in the defiles. After a hair-raising, exhausting march on narrow tracks cut along the side of the cliff-like mountains, he reached Baranis late on 17 April. Chitral was now only 30 miles away but before he could continue his march he would have to devote a day to foraging and resting his tired men.

This day had been a critical one for Robertson and the garrison at Chitral, the culmination of ten days anxiety and strain. On the night of the 7th the lack of vigilance by the Kashmiri sentries had permitted an attempt to set the south-east tower alight. The amount of wood in its construction made it highly inflammable and as the flames flared up into the night sky the fire-fighting parties were silhouetted against the blaze, affording easy targets for the heavy fire poured in by the Chitralis. Luckily, the water supply was still assured and eventually the fire was brought under control, but not before Robertson received a serious wound in the shoulder, an added affliction to the illness he had not yet shaken off. The next night the Chitralis tried again, choosing a moment

A reconnaissance party of Low's division during the advance on Chitral. Note the Gurkha sitting in front.

when the sentries were being changed, but once more the attempt was foiled. Thereafter Townshend made sure that Sikh sentries were always on duty at the most vulnerable points, and devised means to provide a more effective flanking fire along the base of the walls.

The fort's hospital now contained 85 sick and wounded in varying degrees of pain and misery. Hampered by an almost total lack of medical supplies and without suitable nourishment for his patients, Surgeon-Captain Whitchurch did what he could to relieve their suffering during the day; at night he took his turn at sharing the military duties with the other officers, even though his own health was indifferent. The possibility of disease within the narrow confines of the fort caused continual concern and its danger would grow as the weather became hotter. 'The stenches in this awful fort are simply appalling', wrote Townshend in his diary, 'I

feel sick every time I go to inspect.' The crowded conditions, the perpetual jeopardy and uncertainty, the lack of any prospect of early relief, affected everyone to a greater or lesser degree. The morale of the Kashmiri soldiers had never been high, but the British officers always managed to present an optimistic face and Harley's Sikhs generally remained cheerful and dependable, yelling insults at their hated Pathan adversaries.

On the 10th and 11th the watchers on the walls were subjected to frequent alarms, ragged volleys being fired throughout the hours of darkness accompanied by shouting and drumming. An attack seemed imminent, but though none came the tension bred of continual watchfulness further frayed the nerves of men already tired after forty days of siege. On the following day groups of Chitralis were observed making off towards Mastuj, but when evening came the drumming and shouting began afresh. Each consecutive

Type of terrain that confronted Low's troops in the final stages of their advance.

night this continued, until suspicions grew that the noise was a cover to drown the sounds of digging prior to exploding a mine. By the morning of the 17th the noise of picks was unmistakable and it was clear that a tunnel was being dug towards the south-east tower from a summer-house just outside the wall. Since the tunnel seemed only about twelve feet from the wall, a sortie would have to be mounted to destroy it.

The task was given to Harley with 40 of his own Sikhs and 60 Kashmiris. At 4 p.m. the party slipped quietly out of the east gate and made a rush for the summer-house. The Pathan guards were taken completely by surprise but recovered quickly and a fire-fight ensued. The noise brought the Chitralis to their sangars around the fort and the firing between them and the sepoys on the walls grew to a crescendo. Much of this fire impeded operations at the summer-house but Harley organised a covering party to fire

volleys which kept the nearest enemies' heads down. Having discovered the mine shaft, he sent two of his Sikhs down the 50-yard tunnel to ferret out the miners while four more stood ready at the top of the shaft. The Sikhs were in no mood to take prisoners and the luckless tunnellers were bayoneted as they tried to scuttle to safety. Harley himself then placed the explosive charges in the tunnel and lit the fuse, but before it reached the charges two Chitralis, who had remained hidden, broke from cover and scrambled for safety, their feet disconnecting the fuse. Harley had already received urgent messages from Townshend urging him to hurry and the enemy fire outside was growing in intensity, but he could not leave the job unfinished. Seizing a fresh length of fuse he was about to re-enter the tunnel when he was knocked flat by an explosion; the charges had somehow gone off after all. Rallying his men he dashed for the safety of the fort, having

116

been outside for exactly an hour. The tunnel had been burst wide open, 35 of the tunnellers had been bayoneted, several more enemy had been shot, all for the loss of eight men killed and thirteen wounded.

The sortie had been a very risky undertaking but its success saved the fort and raised the spirits of the whole garrison. Robertson was convinced it spelled the end of their troubles and two nights later his certainty was justified, for it was learned that Sher Afzul and his followers had fled and that Muhammad Isa had been defeated at Nisa Gol. When day broke on the 19th a patrol confirmed that not an enemy remained in the sangars or on the hills from which the fort had been harassed for so long. On the following afternoon the sound of bugles was heard and Kelly's war-worn little column was seen winding its way towards the fort, which for twenty-eight days it had striven so valiantly to reach. It was an emotional moment but so tired were the men of both groups after their ordeals that they could only show their relief and thankfulness by a few quiet handshakes — in the undemonstrative way of the late Victorian officer. Robertson and his companions had held out for forty-seven days in a ramshackle fort, with a small force of native troops, of which only a third could be relied upon, on low rations, and without knowledge of when or even if they would be relieved. Twenty years later Townshend, the organiser of the defence, found himself again besieged, this time as a major-general commanding the 6th Indian Division at Kut-el-Amara against the Turks. 'I will hold it as I held Chitral', he said, and he did — for 143 days — but no relief column reached him and he was forced to surrender.

To the south, Gatacre's column of Buffs and Gurkhas had advanced on 18 April but, after five days marching, news of Chitral's deliverance was received and they were ordered to halt until Low caught up with the rest of Gatacre's brigade, leaving the remainder of the division to safeguard the communications rearwards. Snow in the Lowarai Pass and the shortcomings of the track hampered the advance, and it was not until 15 May that the first British troops arrived at Chitral.

Robertson was awarded a knighthood but surprisingly gave up the Indian Political Service in favour of becoming a Liberal MP. Surgeon-Captain Whitchurch won the Victoria Cross for bringing in a dying officer at great risk to his own life during Campbell's ill-fated reconnaissance at the beginning of the siege. Gurdon and Harley received the DSO. Townshend was given the CB and a brevet majority, the same decoration going to Kelly, even though he had been recommended for a KCB and a brevet major-generalship. The importance of his epic march with his stolid but low-caste Mazbi Sikh Pioneers was never fully recognised, most of the publicity and fame for the relief being lavished on Low and his well-known British regiments like the 60th Rifles and Gordon Highlanders.

Umra Khan fled to Afghanistan where he was imprisoned by the Amir while his confederate Sher Afzul was captured and imprisoned in India; both blamed the other for their misfortunes. The boy, Shuja-ul-Mulk, was confirmed as Mehtar of Chitral, and as he grew to manhood proved a sound choice, reigning for 40 years over his people who never gave further trouble. He did, however, have a permanent British garrison to support him, of two Indian battalions with some gunners and sappers, a decision over which there had been much argument. The Indian Government desired it, together with the necessary improvement of the route used by Low's division; this, it was felt, was a strategic necessity imposed by the Russian presence on the Pamirs. The Liberal Government at home ruled against it, largely on grounds of expense. The matter was widely debated and not even eminent soldiers could agree. Roberts and his successor in India, Sir George White, were wholly for it. Sir Neville Chamberlain and Sir Redvers Buller were sceptical of the Russian threat, a view shared by Sir Lepel Griffin, a one-time official of the Punjab Government, who wrote: 'A small Russian detachment might occupy Chitral, but the British Empire would not collapse because a few hundred Cossacks foolishly immured themselves in a death trap.' Then the Liberals lost office and Lord Salisbury, now Prime Minister, decided a garrison should remain at Chitral but the troops at Gilgit should be withdrawn, although a Political Agent remained there, a post subsequently held by Gurdon.

The road north from Peshawar was improved and the Khan of Dir and the Swat tribes induced to protect and maintain it with tribal levies. Permanent garrisons of regulars were placed on the Malakand Pass and at Chakdara Fort on the Swat river. A new and fifth political agency for Dir, Swat and Chitral was established with its headquarters at Malakand under Major Deane, whose skilful negotiations had secured the release of Edwardes and Fowler. Unlike the earlier agencies, who came under the Punjab Government, the agent for Malakand answered direct to the Government of India. Deane's policy aimed at ensuring the peace and tranquillity of his territory with the minimum intervention in the internal affairs of the local tribes. The trade of the Swat Valley prospered, the tribes appeared to welcome a settled and ordered existence, and the new garrisons were left undisturbed. His methods were similar to those of Sandeman in Baluchistan but, in Sir Olaf Caroe's view, Deane's was 'a finer achievement with a more intractable people'. How intractable they could be was proved only twenty-one months after the Malakand agency under Deane was established.

10

The Frontier Ablaze

In June 1896 a Hindu clerk was murdered at a levy post in northern Waziristan. The murderer was never found but a collective fine of 2,000 rupees was imposed on the area concerned; from whom it should be collected was left to the tribal maliks. The inhabitants of Maizar objected to paying their share and much wrangling ensued, until a year later the Political Agent, Mr Gee, rode out to Maizar to settle the dispute. He was accompanied by a military escort of 12 sabres of the 1st Punjab Cavalry, 200 rifles of the 1st Punjab Infantry, 100 of the 1st Sikhs, and two mountain guns, all under command of Lieutenant-Colonel Bunny of the 1st Sikhs.

Regular troops had been garrisoned in Waziristan after an expedition against the Mahsuds in 1895, which had been undertaken as a reprisal for their attack on the Durand Boundary Commission's camp at Wana the year before, following the inclusion of Waziristan in British India. The Mahsuds of southern Waziristan having been quietened, the country had settled down — as much as it ever did — until the murder of the Hindu clerk set in train Mr Gee's visit to Maizar, and a good deal else besides.

When Gee and his troops rode into the village all seemed normal and amicable, and, in the traditions of Pathan hospitality, a meal was offered for the Moslem sepoys of the escort and a shady area under some trees pointed out where the troops could rest. The meal began and the Sikh pipers played. Suddenly a man appeared on a tower waving a sword and two shots rang out, one hitting a subaltern, the other mortally wounding Colonel Bunny, followed by heavy firing from three neighbouring villages. The two guns opened fire with case-shot at the nearest assailants and the infantry were ordered to fall back to a nearby ridge. All the British officers were quickly wounded but the Indian officers rose nobly to the occasion, Subedars Narain Singh and Sundar Singh gallantly covering the retirement, in the course of which the latter and twelve of his sepoys sacrificed their lives to enable the remainder to get clear of the village. Though heavily pressed the little force withdrew with great steadiness, but it was not until evening when reinforcements arrived that they were able to break contact and return to camp.

To punish this murderous outrage the Tochi Field Force of two brigades advanced into the valley in July 1897. Little opposition was met, villages were destroyed but the Wazirs refused to submit. The whole Tochi Valley had to be systematically quartered and it was not until mid-November that they finally came to terms. Earlier appeals for help, both to Kabul and to the Mahsuds, had come to naught, but this had not deterred them from their prolonged intransigence. In this they had been encouraged by events elsewhere.

Ever since the Durand agreement had been signed in 1893, the Amir Abdur Rahman had seemed to regret it. Though he never flouted it, nor gave open encouragement, let alone military support, to his co-religionists on the British side of the border, his stance was sufficiently ambiguous to add fuel to the fires of resentment and distrust increasingly smouldering in the political agencies, as the tribes perceived the implica-

Tribesmen of Waziristan where the Pathan Revolt of 1897 began.

tions of spreading British influence; as they saw it, an influence which could only erode their traditional independence. Whether or not the tribes concluded that they would, sooner or later, receive material support from the Amir is difficult to say. On the other hand, his assumption of the title, 'King of Islam', and his publication and wide distribution of a religious tract stressing the importance of the jehad in the Islamic way of life, cannot but have inflamed the highly devout Pathans. Moreover, even their remote hills did not prevent them learning of British set-backs at the hands of Islam elsewhere. Gordon had been murdered in Khartoum in 1885, and the armies of the Khalifa, the Mahdi's successor, were still triumphant in the Sudan. A massacre of Christians had followed the Sultan of Turkey's victory over the Greeks, and British remonstrances had so infuriated the Sultan that he had sent emissaries to Kabul armed with anti-British propaganda; spreading eastwards, from the mouths of fanatical mullahs, it lost no venom for the hated infidel who was surely ripe for destruction at the hands of the true believer. As these priests — Sadullah, 'the Mad Fakir' from Swat, the Hadda Mullah among the Mohmands, Sayyid Akbar on the Khyber — went about among the tribes, their call for a jehad found a ready response among the Pathans, always susceptible to fanaticism, and increasingly hostile to the boundary stones, the troop movements, the forts that had appeared over the last few years in their hitherto inviolate lands. A storm was about to break over the Frontier on a scale never experienced before. The first rumble was heard where it was least expected, in the best ordered and newest agency — Malakand.

Rumours of possible trouble had reached Deane, the agent, in mid-July. He was of course aware of the outbreak in the Tochi Valley but that was nearly 200 miles away to the south-west. At first he was inclined to discount the rumours, but by 26 July it seemed certain something was going to happen. In garrison on the Malakand Pass was a squadron of the 11th Bengal Lancers (Probyn's Horse), a mountain battery and a company of Madras Sappers and Miners, the 24th and 31st Punjab Infantry and the 45th Sikhs, the latter less 180 men who with 30 sowars of Probyn's occupied Chakdara Fort, ten miles to the north-east. The troops at Malakand occupied a rather extended position, some in the fort on a spur, others in a central camp 700 yards to the north, the rest in another camp 1,300 yards to the north-west. The two camps had low perimeter walls and an abattis but were overlooked by hills on the east and west. In view of the vulnerability of this position, and the detached outposts at Chakdara and at Dargai, at the southern foot of the pass where a

company of the 31st was stationed, the Guides were summoned up from Mardan.

The message reached Mardan at 9 p.m. on the 26th and within three hours, fully equipped with baggage, supplies and ammunition, the Guides were on their way, marching through the night in intense heat. The first 29 miles were on the flat, the last seven a steep climb, by then under a blazing sun. The cavalry reached Malakand in eight hours, the infantry in seventeen and a half; an hour after their arrival they were in action.

At ten on the previous evening a report had come in that the Mad Fakir was approaching from the north-east with a huge following of Swatis. The troops manned their perimeters and Colonel Macrae, 45th Sikhs, sent out a detachment to delay the advance. This small party soon found itself hopelessly outnumbered by swarms of tribesmen, but the Sikhs doggedly disputed every yard as

Colonel Adams and Lieutenant Lord Fincastle winning the Victoria Cross for rescuing Lieutenant Greaves during the action of the Guides Cavalry at Landakai in the Swat valley, 17 August 1897. Water colour by May Dart.

they fell back on the rest of their regiment, which resisted every attack until two in the morning when the enemy pulled back. In the centre fierce hand-to-hand fighting ensued when an assault broke into the sappers' camp and not until just before dawn was the position restored. At daybreak the 31st Punjabis and Probyn's were ordered to follow up the enemy and attempt to make contact with Chakdara, which was also under attack. The Punjabis found their way blocked by masses of enemy but the squadron managed to outflank the latter and reach the fort.

In command of the little garrison of the 45th Sikhs at Chakdara was a subaltern whose name was shared by his regiment after its founder: H.B. Rattray. Having been notified on 23 July of an imminent uprising, he had warned Malakand and was thus himself ready when the attack came in almost simultaneously with that on the main garrison. The assaults were pressed with ferocity all through the night until daylight brought a respite and the welcome arrival of the cavalry. The latter were just in time for the tribes came on again, charging fanatically up to the north and east walls of the fort. Between attacks the garrison endured sniping from a nearby hill which hampered the strengthening of the defences. That night, the 27th, and the next the enemy swarmed forward again, only to be hurled back by close range fire from the Sikhs' Martinis and two Maxims. For the next three days the garrison was under constant pressure, but despite the attackers suffering huge losses nothing seemed to daunt their religious frenzy, as time after time they surged up to the walls. Under frequent heavy attacks and perpetually on the alert, the defenders were growing tired, and on the afternoon of 1 August a simple message was flashed by heliograph to Malakand: 'Help us'.

After enduring equally determined onslaughts on the three successive nights following the first appearance of the tribesmen, the main garrison had tried to relieve Chakdara that very morning, but despite a fine charge by the Guides Cavalry over very broken ground, the column failed to get through and had to retire. Another attempt was made next day which succeeded. After a week's superhuman efforts, the tribesmen suddenly lost heart and made off to their villages. At 10 a.m. the exhausted defenders of Chakdara, recovering from yet another night's savage fighting, threw open the gates to the relief column.

As mentioned earlier, night operations were not generally favoured by tribal forces and massed attacks with knife and sword had grown less common. Yet at Malakand and Chakdara, and indeed on other occasions in 1897, these were not only frequently encountered, but pressed home with great determination and courage. That this was so was ascribed by one military commentator, Captain H.L. Nevill, to the powerful rantings of the mullahs on a susceptible people. Comparing the Pathan attacks in 1897 with those of the Mahdi's followers twelve years before, he wrote: 'There is no instance in the military history of the Egyptians or Sudanese in which temporary insanity brought on by religious fervour has lasted more than 24 hours. Before Malakand and Chakdara the tribesmen were religious maniacs for eight days.' In the face of such prolonged and insensate bravery, not to mention overwhelming numbers, constant vigilance and unyielding discipline were required of the regular troops if they were to hold; this was demonstrated in full measure by the sowars and sepoys of the Malakand garrisons.

Once the extent of the rising was grasped, the Malakand Field Force of two brigades was hastily formed under Major-General Sir Bindon Blood, Low's chief of staff in the Chitral campaign. Advancing up the Swat Valley on 8 August, the submission of the nearmost villages was soon obtained, but at the entrance to Upper Swat, Blood's march was opposed near Landakai. Unused to artillery fire heavier than the mountain batteries, the tribesmen were soon disconcerted by the 12-pounders of 10th Battery, Royal Artillery, and when they found their line of retreat threatened by a turning movement, they disappeared towards the Buner hills, hotly pursued by the sabres and dismounted action

The 13th Bengal Lancers charging the Mohmands at Shabkadr, 6 August 1897. Water colour by E. J. Hobday.

of the Guides Cavalry. The advance continued and by the 24th the Swatis were submitting. Blood now planned to punish the Bunerwals who had come across to join the rising, but more pressing requirements forced him to turn about and march west for Bajaur, where the Utman Khel and Mamunds had come out in direct consequence of an outbreak among their southerly neighbours, the Mohmands.

On 6 August, eleven days after the attack on the Malakand, the Mohmands had attacked the Border Police fort of Shabkadr, 15 miles north of Peshawar. The Police resisted for twelve hours, when the tribesmen drew off at the approach of a small column from Peshawar under Colonel Woon. Owing to difficulties of the ground, Woon's cavalry and guns became separated from his infantry. Seeing their chance, 7,000 Mohmands swooped on the latter, the 20th Punjabis and

part of the 1st Somerset Light Infantry, but in so doing exposed their flank to a surprise charge by the 13th Bengal Lancers. As always when caught in the open by cavalry, the Mohmands broke and fled back to their hills.

Woon's force was now incorporated into the larger Mohmand Field Force under Brigadier-General Elles, who was ordered to march north through Mohmand country in co-operation with Blood's Malakand force coming in from the east. The Mohmands, whose territory had never been fully penetrated by the British, had always been troublesome, always raiding into the Peshawar Valley. In the fifties over a hundred raids had been attributed to them; in the sixties an earlier attack on Shabkadr had been frustrated similarly to the latest one, by a charge of the 7th Hussars; in 1878 they had harassed troops in the Afghan War; and in 1896 they had fought among themselves.

No 3 Mountain Battery, Royal Artillery ready to advance. This battery served with the Mohmand Field Force in September 1897 and subsequently with the Peshawar Moveable Column during the Tirah operations. The gunners are all British, the muleteers Indian.

Now they and their allies to the north were to have their villages burned, their valleys traversed as the two columns pressed inwards to squeeze them into submission.

Using the Panjkora as his start line, Blood advanced westwards on 9 September, Elles from Shabkadr six days later. Leaving one brigade to guard his communications, Blood sent a second under Brigadier-General Jeffries to attack the Utman Khel, while with the third he pushed forward to link up with Elles. This he accomplished by 21 September, but not before having to repulse two severe night attacks on his camp at Nawagai, of which the 1st Queen's bore the brunt. Jeffries, meanwhile, had turned north to punish the Mamunds. Having destroyed several villages, he ordered a retirement. His brigade was in three columns, each out of supporting distance from one another, and sure enough, the Mamunds saw their opportunity, pour-

ing down strongly in pursuit. To relieve the pressure, the 1st Buffs and 35th Sikhs counter-attacked successfully, but when they resumed the withdrawal, the Mamunds came on again and a company of the latter of flank guard found itself isolated and charged at close range. With this company was the correspondent of the *Daily Telegraph*, Lieutenant Winston S. Churchill of the 4th Hussars, who described the scene: 'As the soldiers rose from the shelter of the rocks behind which they had been firing, an officer turned quickly round, his face covered with blood. He put his hands to his head and fell on the ground. Two of the men ran to help him away. One fell shot through the leg. A sepoy who was still firing sprang into the air and, falling, began to bleed terribly. Another fell close to him. Everyone began to pull those men along, dragging them roughly over the rocky ground in spite of their groans.

No 3 Mountain Battery, Royal Artillery in action.

Another officer was immediately shot. Several Sikhs ran forward to his help. Thirty-yards away was the crest of the spur. From this a score of tribesmen were now firing with deadly effect. Over it ran a crowd of swordsmen, throwing pieces of rock and yelling. The two officers who were left used their revolvers. The men fired wildly. One officer and two wounded sepoys were dropped on the ground. The officer lay on his back. A tall man in dirty-white linen pounced on him with a sword. It was a horrible sight. The retreat continued . . . the bullets struck dust spurts all round. Most of the wounded were, however, carried off. At length the bottom of the hill was reached. Then somebody sounded the charge. Bayonets were fixed . . . the officers ran forward and waved their swords. Everyone began to shout. Then the forward movement began — slowly at first, but gaining momentum rapidly. As the enemy fled back . . . many dropped under the fire of the Sikhs.'

The Buffs came up to the rescue and the Guides Infantry were sent to another hard-pressed Sikh company. Eventually, covered by the Buffs firing steady volleys, the force reached camp, as darkness and a thunderstorm came to the aid of the rearguard; it was then discovered that Jefferies himself had been cut off with a handful of troops in a burning village. He survived, but as Churchill said, 'it was an anxious night; perhaps the fitting close to an exciting day.'

It had been a bad start and the enemy had been gravely underestimated. In fact the reduction of the Mamunds was to take another seven weeks, under the direct command of Blood and after reinforcements had arrived. Following Blood's departure, Elles continued operations against the Mohmands, driving them from their positions astride the Badmanai Pass, and by the end of the month the enemy came to terms. A particularly encouraging feature of this phase had been a spirited attack put in by the

The 35th Sikhs fighting a rearguard action against tribesmen during the operations of the Malakand Field Force, possibly the fight with the Mamunds at which Winston Churchill was present. Water colour by E. J. Hobday.

Officers and men of the Khyber Rifles, the irregular corps which failed to hold the Khyber forts in August 1897.

Afridi company of the 20th Punjabis; the significance of this lay in the fact that a month before their fellow tribesmen in the Khyber, who had remained quiet for so long, had risen in revolt, the great pass was closed, and the Pathan revolt had now spread south of the Kabul river.

During Warburton's custodianship of the Khyber, the security of the pass had been upheld by an irregular corps of local levies, the Khyber Rifles, raised by him after the Afghan War; this force, officered entirely by Afridis, maintained garrisons at either end of the pass, Landi Kotal to the west, Fort Maude to the east, and centrally at Ali Masjid. They had always proved reliable, so much so that they had even been employed outside their own area in the Black Mountain expeditions of 1888 and 1891, where they had given good service. Tranquil though the Khyber had remained, there was a flaw in this tranquillity: so much of it depended on the personality of Warburton himself, and in May 1897 he went on leave, pending retirement.

The flames of the jehad ignited among the Swatis and Mohmands by the Mad Fakir and the Hadda Mullah were spreading south, fanned by the mullah Sayyid Akbar among the Orakzais and Afridis. Reports of his activities reached the authorities in the first fortnight of August. The garrisons along the north-south line, Jamrud — Bara — Kohat, were strengthened, while Brigadier-General Yeatman-Briggs assumed command at the last-named, to be ready to act either in the Kurram Valley, or in support of the forts along the Samana Range, west of Kohat, which had been occupied after earlier trouble with the Orakzais in 1891. Nothing, however, was done about the Khyber forts. There were, in any case, few regular troops to spare, the operations in Malakand and the Mohmand country being by then under way, and it was also felt that nothing should be done which might imply distrust of the Khyber Afridis in general and the Khyber Rifles in particular.

Sadly, such trust was misplaced. On 23 August, seventeen days after the attack on Shabkadr, the Afridis struck. The Khyber Rifles at Ali Masjid abandoned the fort without a fight. Their comrades at Fort Maude resisted for some while but then fell back on a rescue force sent out from Jamrud. The next day Landi Kotal was attacked. Its garrison of 370 men held out for 24 hours but then treachery struck from within. Some disloyal elements joined the attackers, the fort fell, and the loyal troops had to fight their way through to safety at Jamrud. The pass was to remain in hostile hands for four months.

Having held their hand until they saw how the Afridis had fared, the Orakzais rose on 26 August, striking first near Kohat and then, at the beginning of September further west in the Kurram Valley, where they were joined by some Afridis. Yeatman-Briggs took out a column to restore order but on the 11th he had to march against a large force massing to attack the Samana Range. Having driven them away, he was forced by shortage of water to return to his base. Observing his retirement the Afridis and Orakzais redoubled their efforts against the Samana forts.

The range ran due east-west and was held by regular troops of the 36th Sikhs divided between two forts, Gulistan to the west and Lockhart four miles away to the east, the latter having an outpost of 41 men two miles further east at Sangar. Communications between Gulistan and Lockhart were maintained by a heliograph station sited midway between them at Saragarhi, defended by a

havildar and 20 sepoys. On the morning of 12 September all these posts were attacked. Sangar and Lockhart held out but the tiny garrison at Saragarhi was hopelessly outnumbered. Undaunted, the handful of Sikhs threw back two determined assaults during the morning, inflicting heavy casualties. Unfortunately, there was, near the base of one of the towers, a patch of dead ground in which some Afridis concealed themselves and worked away at the brickwork until a hole was made, bringing down the masonry. Into the breach so made the tribesmen poured, as the Sikhs rushed from the walls to stem the onslaught. Forced back to their living quarters, Havildar Ishar Singh and his few men fought on until 4.30 in the afternoon, when the last survivors were overwhelmed and killed.

The triumphant Afridis made off to swell the numbers which had meanwhile been surrounding Fort Gulistan. This was held by

Fort Ali Masjid, abandoned by the Khyber Rifles to the Afridis and not retaken until December 1897.

The ruins of the signal post at Saragarhi on the Samana Range, defended by 21 men of the 36th Sikhs until overwhelmed on 12 September 1897. Photograph taken after its recapture with Sikhs lining the walls.

165 men of the same regiment under Major Des Voeux, whose concern for the safety of his post was heightened by the presence therein of his wife and family, together with his children's nurse. The fort had been invested since the morning, and though the fate of Saragarhi had been visible from the walls, so great were the enemy numbers in between that nothing could be done to save its heroic garrison. On being reinforced after its fall, the attackers of Gulistan poured up in strength to positions, also in dead ground, close to the west wall. Fire could not be brought to bear upon them, so a sortie was made with great daring by two havildars and 28 sepoys. Though over half were killed or wounded, they succeeded in driving the enemy away. Nevertheless, the attacks continued over the next two days and it was not until the 15th, when the gunfire of Yeatman-Briggs' column advancing from Fort Lock-

hart began to fall among the surrounding hordes, that the defenders knew relief was at hand. Faced by fresh troops the tribesmen gave up the siege and the Samana range was once more in British hands. For their stout-hearted defence of these posts the 36th Sikhs were later awarded the battle-honour 'Samana', a distinction held by no other regiment, British or Indian, and a memorial was raised to honour the men who had held Saragarhi until overcome.

Although Blood's operations against the Mamunds were still going on and would continue to do so for at least another month, it was now decided to punish the Afridis and Orakzais by an invasion of their summer home in the Tirah Maidan, a wide valley running east-west enclosed by roughly parallel ridges, of which the southern-most was the Samana, and the most northerly, the mighty Safed Koh range running from the

129

Peiwar Kotal in the west almost to Fort Bara in the east: a region never hitherto entered by British troops. Since Afridi territory covered some 900 square miles and since the Afridis and Orakzais combined could muster between 40–50,000 fighting men, a large force, the largest ever employed on the Frontier, had to be assembled: British, Indian, Gurkha and Imperial Service troops (from the princely states) coming up from all over India, even as far away as Madras.

The striking force for the Tirah consisted of two divisions, each of two brigades and divisional troops — two squadrons of cavalry, three mountain batteries, a sapper company, a regiment of pioneers, a battalion of Imperial Service infantry and field hospitals. Each brigade had two British battalions, one Indian and one Gurkha. In support of these two divisions was a very strong brigade to guard the lines of communication, another in reserve at Rawalpindi, and two more of varying strength forming the Peshawar and Kurram Moveable Columns to assist on the flanks. The entire Tirah Field Force, under the command of Lieutenant-General Sir William Lockhart, numbered 11,892 British officers and men, 22,614 Indian or Gurkha, and nearly 20,000 non-combatants. A proclamation issued before operations began stated, in stark terms, that the force would 'march through the country of the Afridis

Types of the 36th Sikhs in 1897, the regiment which defended the Samana forts against the Afridis.

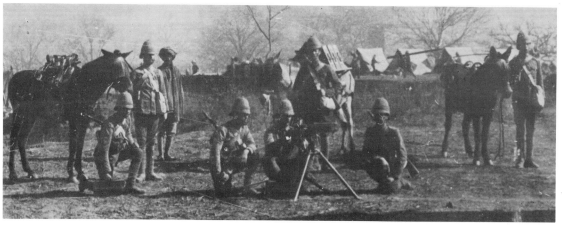

The Maxim gun detachment of the 16th Lancers, part of the divisional troops of Major-General Yeatman-Briggs' 2nd Division of the Tirah Field Force.

Piper Findlater, 1st Battalion Gordon Highlanders, winning the Victoria Cross at the storming of the Dargai Heights, 20 October 1897. Painting by Vereker Hamilton.

and the Orakzais and announce from the heart of the country the final terms which would be imposed. The advance is made to mark the fact that these tribes took part in the attacks [on the Khyber and around Kohat] and the power of the British Government to advance if and when they choose.' Usually erring tribes were given a time by which they could submit if they so preferred rather than accept punishment, but not so on this occasion. In any case, it was unlikely that a tribe of the Afridis' calibre would have tamely knuckled under.

Lockhart's plan was to advance from Kohat where the force concentrated and enter Tirah from the south by crossing the Samana Range at a kotal west of Fort Gulistan and forcing the intervening passes of Sampagha and Arhanga which afforded entry into the Tirah Maidan itself. Leaving Kohat on 11th October, Yeatman-Briggs' 2nd Division in the lead had the task of seizing the kotal. Near the top of the almost precipitous ridge stood the village of Dargai,* approachable only by a very steep, narrow footpath, between which and the kotal was a bare, open slope forming a glacis some 300 yards long, which was entirely commanded by the village and the sangars along the heights at a range of less than 500 yards. On 18 October, while Kempster's 3rd Brigade made an encircling move to threaten the enemy's line of retreat, the 3rd Gurkhas supported by the 2nd King's Own Scottish Borderers of Westmacott's 4th Brigade moved to the attack. Perhaps apprehensive of the threat to their rear — although Kempster was badly delayed by the terrain — the

*No connection with the place of the same name near Malakand.

131

Bombay Sappers and Miners in the Arhanga Pass, Tirah Field Force.

Orakzais holding the ridge did not await the final assault and Dargai was taken for a loss of ten killed and 53 wounded. Kempster's men did not appear until after 3 p.m., by which time several thousand Afridis were observed advancing from the north. Since it was thought there was insufficient time to prepare the position for defence; since the troops on the ridge had no supplies, firewood or warm clothing to endure the cold night, and there was no water nearer than three miles away; and in view of the Afridis coming on, and the 1st Division being out of supporting range, it was decided not to risk holding the position gained, and the two brigades withdrew down the way they had come — not without harassment from the rapidly advancing and doubtless jubilant Afridis. The comments of the men in the ranks who had done the work are not on record but can well be imagined.

On the 20th, therefore, the whole busi-ness had to be done again but by now there were some 12,000 Afridis on the heights in strongly built sangars, their standards bravely mocking the troops far below. The 1st Division had come up, but since the 2nd knew the ground, again it was they, or rather Kempster's brigade, with the 2nd Derbyshire* and 3rd Sikhs attached from the 1st Division, who had to carry the position. Covered by the divisional artillery and an extra battery, the 1st/2nd Goorkhas† led the attack, supported by the 1st Dorsetshire and the Derbys. All went well until the open glacis was reached. Across this the enemy fire was so intense, that despite heroic efforts, only three companies of Gurkhas were able to reach the far side where they had to take cover in dead ground. The mountain guns redoubled their

*Later Sherwood Foresters (Notts and Derby).

†This regiment has always retained this form of 'Gur-kha' in its title.

132

fire but their nine-pounder shells had little effect on the Afridi sangars which had overhead cover. Again and again the 2nd Goorkhas tried to reach their comrades across the fire-swept slope. The Dorsets tried, the Derbys tried, but all to no avail. It seemed impossible to survive on that death-trap of a glacis. After five hours struggle, Kempster decided to use fresh troops.

Then occurred one of the most famous attacks on the Frontier, one that would thrill the newspaper-reading public at home, fill the pages of patriotic books for boys, even be re-enacted on the music-halls. In command of the 1st Gordon Highlanders was Lieutenant-Colonel Mathias. Forming his battalion for the attack, he called out: 'Highlanders! The general says the position must be taken at all costs. The Gordons will take it!' Three minutes concentrated gunfire rained down on the sangars, the pipers struck up *Cock o' the North*, and the Gordons surged forward as one man. Many dropped, among them Piper Findlater shot through both ankles; despite his wounds and his exposed position he piped on, cheering his comrades. With bayonets glinting in the bright sunlight, they charged across the glacis, past the trapped Gurkhas, and on, up the narrow twisting path, scrambling ever higher towards the muzzle flashes in the sangars, while all the way, above the shouts and yells, the crash and rattle of musketry, the pipes screamed their ancient rant. Close on their heels came the bearded sepoys of the 3rd Sikhs, and behind them Gurkhas, Dorsets and Derbys. As the dark green kilts came nearer and nearer, the Afridis knew it was time to go and everywhere gave way. Soon the Highlanders crowned the heights and Dargai was won. Thirty-six men had been killed and 159 wounded, some of the latter seriously; the casualties among officers had been disproportionately high, almost all occurring at the start of the glacis as they had given a lead to their men. Colonel Mathias, himself wounded, and Piper Findlater were subsequently awarded the Victoria Cross.

Several days were now spent reconnoitring forward, foraging for supplies and improving

the tracks. Although no major resistance was offered by the enemy, not a day passed without some attack, particularly on small parties or when troops were retiring, and not a night without long-range sniping into the camp. When the advance was resumed, carefully planned assaults were mounted against both the Sampagha and Arhanga Passes, but the terrain proved a greater obstacle than the enemy opposition which, compared to Dargai, was slight; attributable in Lockhart's view to the hard lesson inflicted on the tribesmen in the first action that even their strongest positions could be forced.

On 1 November the force set up camp in the beautiful and fertile Tirah Maidan. Normally well-populated, the valley was now deserted, though the continuing harassment

1st Battalion Northamptonshire Regiment evacuating their wounded under fire when trapped in the nullah after the withdrawal from Saran Sar, 9 November 1897. Drawing by Melton Prior, correspondent of the Illustrated London News *with the Tirah Field Force.*

Burning a village in the Tirah Maidan.

of picquets, foraging parties and scouting detachments showed that the tribesmen were still active in the surrounding hills, waiting their chance to pounce upon the unwary or ill-protected. The movement forward of the force's baggage train was particularly liable to a swift and bloody onset. In one such foray a small escort of the 1st Queen's was ambushed at dusk, losing three men killed and four wounded, some rifles, a quantity of ammunition and 350 soldiers' kits; had not a detachment of the 1st Northamptonshire come out to the rescue, the whole party would have been butchered.

The chief perpetrators of these raids and the nightly fusillades were the Zakha Khel, the most powerful and numerous of the Afridi clans. The Orakzais were by now showing indications of their willingness to submit, following the issue of notices summoning the tribal jirgas to hear the terms on which the field force was prepared to evacuate the

Tirah. By the end of November the Orakzais had paid the levied fines — both in rifles and in cash — but the Zakha Khel and the smaller clans which they were able to coerce continued the fight.

How dangerous they could be was demonstrated during the various expeditions Lockhart now instituted to penetrate every quarter of the Tirah. On 9 November, for instance, a reconnaissance in force was made to the high peak of Saran Sar, commanding the eastern end of the Tirah Maidan, by a strong brigade under Westmacott of the 1st Dorsets, 1st Northamptons, 15th and 36th Sikhs with two mountain batteries. While the 15th Sikhs escorted the guns, the other three battalions began the ascent to the ridge line. Overcoming some slight opposition, the Northamptons in the centre and the 36th Sikhs on their right reached the crest by late morning, although the Dorsets were held up by some firing and the difficult nature of the ground.

134

Nevertheless, the necessary reconnaissances and surveying of the country beyond were completed without interference by midday, and Westmacott was about to withdraw when the arrival of Lockhart and his staff delayed the rearward movement. Eventually the staffs went back and the 36th Sikhs took up an intermediate position in the rear to cover the withdrawal of the rearguard, five companies of the Northamptons. As these gradually pulled back in their turn, the last company came under heavy fire from a wooded spur to its left, suffering several casualties. Since wounded could never be left behind, this company had to hold its ground while the casualties were evacuated, a slow and difficult task on steep, rocky ground, requiring four men to each stretcher, all of which caused further delay. However, supported by the Sikhs, the task was done and the last company rejoined its battalion. Once the Northamptons were clear, the Sikhs withdrew by a separate route, covering what was now the left flank of the retirement. Assuming his right to be covered by the Dorsets, and since the presence of the wounded was slowing down his march, Colonel Chaytor commanding the Northamptons chose the shortest and easiest route back to camp, which was a ravine or nullah up which they

Announcing terms to Orakzai maliks at a jirga held at Sir William Lockhart's camp in the Maidan. Lockhart is the officer in the dark tunic, back to camera.

135

had advanced that morning. On entering the nullah the leading companies pushed on, leaving the rear three to bring on the wounded. There were only four miles to go but dusk was falling. Suddenly a mass of Afridis appeared on the edge of the nullah, opening fire at close range, picking off the stretcher parties first. The Northamptons were caught in a trap, as *The Times* correspondent, Colonel Hutchinson, described: 'Surrounded by the enemy, exposed to a galling fire from the high banks to which they could not effectively reply, with dead and dying men on every side, and the horror of their desperate situation accentuated by the gathering darkness, they fought on resolutely and bravely, and sacrificed themselves without hesitation to protect and save if possible their wounded comrades who could not help themselves.' The timely return of a Sikh company to their aid enabled most of the trapped men to escape from that deadly nullah, but their rearmost detachment, under Lieutenant MacIntyre, were killed to a man as they covered the withdrawal.

Colonel Chaytor received some censure for his choice of route, but the incident revealed what could happen to battalions pitched into a major Frontier campaign without prior experience of tribal fighting. Unlike the Gordons and Scottish Borderers who had been through the Chitral campaign, the Northamptons and Dorsets had joined the Tirah Field Force direct from quiet garrisons in central and southern India. A week later, during another retirement, a Dorset company found itself in an almost identical situation, losing two officers and 19 killed and wounded after being ambushed in a darkening defile. The British infantry may have lacked the tactical expertise of the more experienced Sikhs and Gurkhas, but there was no doubting their tenacity and coolness under fire. An eyewitness said of the Northamptons' fight: 'the way in which they stuck to their wounded and brought them through that terrible defile was a display of heroism and devotion worthy of a regiment that fought at Albuera.'*

A demonstration of how the Afridis' speed and ardour in pursuit could be turned against them was given on the same ground a

*As 48th Foot in 1811, during the Peninsular War.

The 2nd Punjab Infantry in action against tribesmen, 1897. Water colour by C. J. Staniland.

Maxim gun detachment of 2nd Battalion King's Own Yorkshire Light Infantry, the regiment which distinguished itself in support of the 36th Sikhs at Shin Kamar on 29 January 1898.

few days later. Since the start of the campaign specially selected companies of Gurkhas had been attached to brigades as scouts. Being as natural hill-fighters as the Pathans, the Gurkha scouts had proved a most worthwhile innovation, particularly in countering the Afridis' nocturnal activities by ambushing and stalking snipers. On the day in question the scout companies of the 3rd and 5th Gurkhas provided the rearguard for the second retirement from Saran Sar. Having warned the battalion in position to their rear, they delayed the Afridi advance for a time but then abandoned their positions at such speed that the Afridis, thinking they were in flight, followed up without any caution, only to come under a decimating crossfire from the rearward battalion — a reverse which allowed the retirement to proceed without any hindrance.

Throughout November and into the first week of December columns marched out to 'show the flag' in every part of the Tirah and destroy the villages and supplies of the recal-

citrant. As stated earlier, the Orakzais made submission, but only a few of the Afridi clans came in to seek terms, the Zakha Khel and others remaining obdurate. However, the winter snows were now approaching, and since even the Afridis left the Maidan in winter, to keep a force there would be out of the question and it was decided to evacuate. Lockhart's plan was to withdraw eastwards down the roughly parallel Bara and Waran valleys which ultimately joined near Barkai, ten miles south-west of Fort Bara, destroying all still-rebellious villages en route. When the force was re-united he intended to re-deploy around Barkai — Bara — Jamrud, so as to dominate the winter homes of the Afridis in the lower Bara and Bazar valleys, and re-open the Khyber which lay to the north of the latter.

The evacuation began on 7 December, the 1st Division taking the southerly Waran route, the 2nd down the Bara. The former encountered very slight resistance and a week later had reached Fort Bara without difficulty, leaving a trail of burning villages to mark its passage. The 2nd Division's march began in appalling weather, bitterly cold, alternate rain and snow, with thick mists hampering the withdrawal of the flanking picquets. To add to the difficulties, the march was subject to constant attack, not only on the rearguard, but along the whole length of the column from front to rear, with detachments being cut off and delayed by their wounded, so that parties had to be sent back to rescue them. The cold and sudden ambushes particularly unnerved the unarmed non-combatants many of whom decamped so that soldiers had to be told off to carry the wounded. The Afridis fought with great fanaticism, especially on the 13th, the last day of the withdrawal. Before the 4th Brigade in the rear could even clear the previous night's camp, the enemy appeared in great strength. Covered by the divisional guns, and after inflicting heavy losses, the rearguard — Scottish Borderers, 36th Sikhs and 3rd Gurkhas — managed to break contact, but were soon hard pressed again in fighting that continued for so long that the three battalions had to remain holding a ridge across the route all through the bitter night without food or blankets. When they fell back in the morning, the tribesmen followed up closely until the exhausted rearguard came under protection of fresh picquets established by the Peshawar Column which had advanced from Fort Bara. Both brigades then encamped at Barkai, having suffered 164 casualties during the five days and nights of their fighting withdrawal.

The 2nd Division were now left to recover from their exertions and watch the mouth of the Bara valley, as the 1st Division and the Peshawar Column were concentrated at Jamrud. While the 1st Division penetrated the Bazar valley with only slight skirmishing, the latter marched through the Khyber as far as Landi Kotal, restoring the forts. By 1 January 1898, Lockhart had three brigades holding the Khyber from Landi Kotal to Jamrud, and two more poised on the northeast border of Afridi territory. A concentric advance from Ali Masjid, Jamrud and Bara to capture a herd of Afridi cattle drew blank and the operation ended in a minor tragedy. One of the regiments most distinguished in the whole campaign had been the 36th Sikhs, under the inspiring leadership of Colonel Haughton. During its withdrawal from the Shin Kamar Pass under fire, a misunderstanding led to the premature removal of a picquet holding a vital knoll covering the line of retreat. Two companies of the 2nd King's Own Yorkshire Light Infantry were sent forward to retake it, but before they could do so, came under heavy fire at close range, losing a number of men and becoming pinned down. Haughton went to their aid with part of his regiment, but so encumbered with wounded were both detachments, and so fierce the attack, that no further retirement was possible. Urgent messages for reinforcements went back but, before any could arrive, Haughton himself was killed leading a charge to try to cover the removal of the wounded. It was a gallant end but a sad loss of a most outstanding officer, and tragic that it should have come about in a regiment whose steadiness in action had so often saved others. On the other hand, the Yorkshire Light Infantry emerged with credit for their cool determination in what had been their first action of the campaign and a testing one at that.

Apart from some simultaneous actions away to the north-east where the delayed punishment of the Bunerwals was being pursued by Sir Bindon Blood, the military operations of the great Pathan revolt were at an end. From Swat to Tochi the cease-fire sounded along the Frontier, the tribes began to rebuild their shattered villages and the British to count the cost. Several millions had been spent and the Tirah force alone had suffered over a thousand casualties. Although the military objectives had ultimately been achieved, the field forces had been untrained and inexperienced as fighting formations, and more than once commanders and staffs had been saved by the courage and discipline of the troops. As one military historian of the Frontier, Major-General Elliott, has pointed out, 'the army learnt the

Fort Jamrud as it appeared in 1897. Compare with its appearance in 1865 on page 17.

lesson that it is not enough to assemble the component parts of a force from the four corners of the Punjab and expect it to march triumphantly into, and out of, battle.'

It had been fortunate that the independence of the tribes one from another had permitted neither any sort of unified conduct of their operations, nor even an entirely simultaneous uprising. Furthermore, although the torch of revolt originally lit in the Tochi Valley may have sparked off the risings to the north, the subsequent presence of troops in Tochi had formed a protective screen between the Tirah and the Mahsuds of southern Waziristan, the most formidable tribe of all, who never came out in the revolt. Their turn, however, would come. Politically the campaign had solved nothing. The rebellious tribes had been chastened, but the underlying grievances and apprehensions behind the insurrection remained unresolved. The resentment continued, as evinced by the Afridis who, despite the fire and sword carried through their valleys, took their time in making their submissions. By dint of political activity and Lockhart's personal influence with them, they eventually did so, the Zakha Khel being the last to come in in early April.

Alongside their recalcitrance, on the other hand, was revealed a strange quirk of the Pathan character. When Lockhart left Peshawar for leave in England, he was seen off by hundreds of cheering Afridis, Zakha Khel among them, begging to draw his carriage to the station, and vowing that in future they would fight on the British side. Was this a genuine demonstration of goodwill for a man they had come to regard as a worthy opponent, or was their enthusiasm merely a sign of relief at the departure of one who had grievously ravaged their homes? Despite the protestations of future friendship, despite the submissions made, the Zakha Khel Afridis would continue to be a thorn in British flesh for the next ten years, and the modern mind might regard demonstrations like that at Peshawar station with more scepticism than did Lockhart's contemporaries. Yet the words of Sir Olaf Caroe should be recalled: 'Englishmen and Pathans looked each between the eyes, and there they found — a man. Sometimes the pledge they made was broken; there were wild men and fanatics, and on one side the assassin struck, on the other the avenger. But the pledge held, the respect, the affection survived.'

139

11

The Superior Viceroy

My name is George Nathaniel Curzon
I am a most superior person,
My cheek is pink, my hair is sleek
I dine at Blenheim once a week.

Thus did an Oxford undergraduate mockingly describe his contemporary, who twenty years later became Governor-General of India, the youngest man bar one ever to hold that high office. Superior he remained, in manner, in intellect, in capacity for hard work, though underlying his impressive demeanour was an easily wounded sensitivity. Never had India received a Governor-General, or Viceroy as the post was now usually called, who had prepared himself so conscientiously for his task, one on which he had set his heart since his boyhood at Eton. On entering Parliament in 1886 his main concern had been the study of foreign affairs, particularly those of Asia whereof he conceived India to be the mainspring. In 1891 he became Under-Secretary at the India Office in Lord Salisbury's Conservative Government, and four years later Under-Secretary at the Foreign Office, where he made his parliamentary reputation. When out of office or during the parliamentary recesses he travelled extensively to equip himself for his intended task, visiting Persia, Central Asia, Afghanistan and India itself.

Arriving as Viceroy on 3 January 1899, his quick enquiring mind, his rapid judgements, his enthusiasm and persistence, above all his industry, soon galvanised the bureaucracy of the Indian Government into an unprecedented activity which it was neither accustomed to nor particularly well-designed for. This is not the place to consider the many reforms Curzon initiated during his term of office except for one: the removal of responsibility for the Frontier from the Punjab Government, and the creation of a new North-West Frontier Province, directly responsible to the Government of India.

It had long been apparent that the administration of the Frontier by the Lieutenant-Governor of the Punjab had presented certain anomalies, particularly since the adoption of the forward policy which had entailed the occupation of the Khyber, Kurram, parts of Waziristan and Malakand, and the demarcation of the Durand Line. The problem had been the existence of two bands of territory: on the one hand the settled districts under the Commissioners of Peshawar and the Derajat between the Indus and the old administrative border; on the other, the tribal territory beyond the latter where a looser form of control was maintained. However, since the peoples of both territories were more or less homogeneous, with close connections of race, marriage and trade necessitating constant movement across the administrative border in both directions, the administration of the two, though different, became inextricably linked. Even more anomalous was the external affairs aspect. Here was a highly volatile area, difficult to control, but whose security was vital to that of India as a whole for which the Government of India was responsible. Yet, between the Frontier and the central government was placed a subordinate government, of the Punjab, through whose hands all frontier matters passed — a system fraught with possible delays and disagreements.

After the Pathan revolt, and before Curzon's arrival, a compromise was instituted whereby the Commissioners of Peshawar and the Derajat, while remaining under the Punjab Government for all ordinary administration, should be responsible to the central government in all their dealings with the tribes between the administrative and political borders. Curzon thought little of this, anticipating that the Punjab Government, slighted by such diminution of its authority, would do little to assist and plenty to obstruct the policies of the central government in this area. 'There is not another country in the world', he wrote to the British Cabinet, 'which adopts a system so irrational in theory, so bizarre in practice, as to interpose between its foreign minister and his most important sphere of activity the barrier, not of a subordinate official, but of a subordinate government.' Curzon got his way, though not without incurring the bitter enmity of Mackworth Young, the Lieutenant-Governor of the Punjab, whom he did not see fit to consult before submitting his proposals to the Secretary of State for India.

Under Curzon's scheme, effective from 9 November 1901, the settled districts were separated from the Punjab to form, with the Political Agencies of Malakand, Khyber, Kurram, Tochi and Wana, and other tribal territory up to the Durand Line, the North-West Frontier Province. This was placed in the charge of a Chief Commissioner who was to be appointed by, and directly responsible to, the Government of India, for the administration of the districts and political control of the tribal belt. The first incumbent was Harold Deane, who had formed the Malakand agency.

Concurrent with the establishment of the province came a new security policy. The antagonisms caused among the tribes by the forward policy which had led to the 1897 uprisings had not been alleviated when Curzon arrived. He found 10,000 regular troops still stationed beyond the administrative border in Malakand, the Khyber, on the Samana range and in Waziristan; plans were in hand for the construction of costly fortifica-

Lord Curzon, Viceroy of India 1899–05, and Lady Curzon.

tions in tribal territory. Not only were these deployments antagonistic, they were also inefficient, with garrisons dispersed far from their bases and without lateral communications. Curzon reversed all this in favour of a new arrangement, the ingredients of which he summarised as: 'withdrawal of British forces from advanced positions, employment of tribal forces in defence of tribal territory, concentration of British forces in British territory behind them as a safeguard and a support, improvement of communications in the rear.'

Some of the tribal forces, like the Khyber Rifles, had existed for some time, and others, like the Kurram, Zhob, North and South Waziristan Militias, Chitral Scouts, came into being, all being placed on a proper military footing under British officers seconded from the Indian Army. Controlled by the Political Agents and formed into wings each of 500 lightly-armed infantrymen, the Militias were stationed in forts from which smaller garrisons were found for outlying posts; mobile patrols of platoon

141

Lord Kitchener of Khartoum, Commander-in-Chief India, 1902–09.

strength went out daily to quarter their territory and hunt down raiders or other malefactors. If they encountered trouble with which they could not cope, support would have to be summoned from the regular troops providing moveable columns from such places as Malakand, Peshawar, Kohat and Bannu, for which the Militias would then scout, collect information and protect the flanks. Operating entirely within tribal territory, their duties nevertheless brought them into contact with a second, para-military force in the settled districts, the Border Military Police, which was later reconstituted as a more efficient body, the Frontier Constabulary, whose officers were seconded from the Indian Police. This constabulary was not permitted to cross the administrative border unless in hot pursuit of criminals.

Behind these forces stood the Army in India and here too a reforming hand was at work. At Curzon's specific request there arrived in 1902 as Commander-in-Chief India a figure as imposing as himself, Lord Kitchener of Khartoum, who had just brought the South African War to a close. Kitchener was unimpressed by what he found and completely disagreed with the idea, then current in India, that 'the Army is intended to hold India against the Indians'. The dispersion of units all over the sub-continent in small, localised garrisons was inefficient, provided poor training for war, as had been seen in 1897, and was bad for morale, particularly for those regiments in the hot, placid south. Kitchener set out four main principles: that the Army's chief role was the defence of the North-West Frontier against external aggression; that its organisation should be the same in peace as in war; that the internal security role was secondary and chiefly the task of the police, in whose support troops might nevertheless have to act at times; and that all units should have experience and training on the terrain where they might be called upon to perform in their chief role, the Frontier.

Kitchener envisaged nine fighting divisions ready for war, grouped in two commands, each on the main axes to the Frontier: five in the north on the line Lucknow — Peshawar — Khyber, and four in the south, Bombay — Mhow — Quetta. In the event this plan had to be modified due to building costs entailed by the new deployments, but the nine divisions were formed and units allotted to them so that, on mobilisation, each would contain, besides its infantry brigades and supporting artillery, a cavalry brigade and additional troops for internal security. To avoid localisation and to give all units experience of the Frontier, the units were rotated between divisions after some years, the divisional locations remaining constant.

As a further means of abolishing localisation and emphasising that in future there was to be one Indian Army, the old designations of Bengal, Madras and Bombay were dropped from regimental titles, and all cavalry and infantry regiments were renumbered in a single sequence for each arm, only the Gurkhas remaining outside this numbering. One consequence of Kitchener's policy was the disbandment of the Punjab Frontier Force as a separate formation, its regiments becoming part of the Indian Army as a whole, though permitted to retain the words 'Frontier Force' as part of their individual designations. The loss of the PFF, or 'Piffers' as they were known, after so many years invaluable and highly skilled service on the Frontier caused controversy and bitterness which lasted for many years, but there is no doubt that Kitchener's reorganisation of the Army in India was urgently required and did much to modernise a force which, within a decade, would be called upon to fight, not in defence of the Frontier, but against great armies in

Sowar of the 9th Bengal Lancers (Hodson's Horse), circa 1900

France and the Middle East.

Both Curzon and Kitchener had been fully seized of the threat posed to India's frontiers by Russia, whose strategic railway system in Central Asia had continued to grow and who again was intending to send emissaries to the Amir of Afghanistan. At the turn of the century, with Britain gravely embroiled in South Africa and British troops being sent from the Indian garrisons to that theatre, Russia's traditional inclination to apply leverage on Britain elsewhere by threatening India was greatly enhanced. From 1901 the threat seemed graver, not on the North-West Frontier, but north of the Himalayas; three years later this determined Curzon to despatch an expedition to Tibet to forestall Russian encroachments in that country. However, by then Russia's attention was transferred to the Far East where she went to war with Japan, with whom Britain had signed an alliance in 1902. Despite Russia's surprising and crushing defeat by the Japanese, the authorities in India were still

143

A rearguard action by the 4th Gurkhas, circa 1910. Water colour by A. C. Lovett.

Jirga held by Major-General Willcocks to impose terms upon the Zakha Khel Afridis at the close of the Bazar Valley operations in 1908.

concerned about the railway network in Central Asia which, it was calculated, could poise 60,000 men against India's frontiers within two months of any outbreak of hostilities. Furthermore, if Russia persevered with her intentions of establishing a presence in Kabul, Britain's supervision of Afghanistan's foreign affairs, agreed by the treaty concluded with Abdur Rahman, would be seen to be hollow. Abdur Rahman had died in 1901, being succeeded by his son, Habibulla, whom Curzon wished to press for a firm pro-British commitment, but the British Government saw more advantage in a neutral Afghanistan and, overruling Curzon, concluded a treaty with Habibulla on similar lines to the previous one.

Then suddenly the Great Game — the long struggle for supremacy in Central Asia — petered out. The intrigues with distant khans, hurried journeys of secret agents, covert surveys of unmapped routes, the contingency plans for conquest or control, the diplomatic exchanges, all had finally run their course; the long-imagined confrontation between Cossack and Sowar in the passes ceased to haunt the minds of soldiers and politicians in London and St Petersburg, in Simla and Tashkent. To Russia's discomfiture at her defeat by Japan was added a growing concern of the new threat posed in Europe by Germany. Anglo-Russian talks were opened to discuss Persia, Afghanistan and Tibet, and in 1907 a Convention was signed. Both countries agreed to refrain from intervention in Tibet, Persia was divided into spheres of influence, while as for Afghanistan Russia accepted it as being within Britain's sphere, and Britain undertook not to interfere in its internal affairs. Moreover, Britain and Russia, for so long potential enemies, now found themselves linked together through their separate alliances with France in the face of common danger, the Kaiser.

Indian service dress as worn by 2nd Battalion 60th Rifles, 1909. From left: light marching order; heavy marching order; scout order.

145

By the time the Anglo-Russian Convention was signed, Curzon had left India, a broken and disappointed man. The brilliance and achievements of his early years as Viceroy had been tarnished by personal distress, increasing disagreements with colleagues, and finally a wounding row with Kitchener over the military representation on the Viceroy's Council. Rather than yield to Kitchener he offered his resignation, which was accepted. A term of office which had begun with such high hopes ended in recriminations and hostility.

Whatever else Curzon achieved or failed to achieve in India, there is no doubt that he set his mark on the Frontier by his creation of the new Province. His motives for doing so were inspired chiefly by the needs of foreign policy rather than the welfare of its people, but in Sir Olaf Caroe's view, its greater and more lasting importance lay in the fact that, by separating the Frontier from the Punjab, by whom it had been ruled for so long, in the Sikh era as well as the British, its Pathan inhabitants were given a focus for their own pride, a sense of oneness as a people, and a heightened consciousness that their lives were of concern, not merely to a provincial government, but to the larger responsibilities of the Viceroy himself. By so doing it helped

Men of the 1st Battalion Seaforth Highlanders halted for a meal during the Mohmand Expedition of 1908. Note the Wolseley helmets and Bandolier equipment which have replaced the patterns worn during the Tirah campaign.

to draw the settled districts and the tribal territory together, thus aiding the consolidation of the Frontier.

For his part Curzon claimed that for seven years not a single frontier expedition had had to be mounted; that never before, since Britain assumed control, had such a period been free of the old policy of 'butcher and bolt'. While it is true that nothing on the scale of Ambela, Chitral or the Tirah had been required, and that the settled districts had remained quiet, it had not been so in tribal territory. The Mahsuds, it will be remembered, had taken no part in the 1897 uprising, but from 1898 onwards, under the leadership of the firebrand Mullah Powindah, described by Kitchener as that 'Pestilential Priest', they began to make up for their passivity. Raids across the administrative border, attacks on militia and police posts, ambushes of convoys, murders of political officers, incitement of fellow-Mahsud sepoys of the Militia, there seemed no end to the lawlessness and fear provoked by the Mullah Powindah in the first decade of the new century. Having been disarmed by the Indian Arms Act, the villagers of the settled districts could not defend themselves, and the Border Police, less well-armed than the tribesmen and in fear of reprisals, were ineffective. When a fine of £10,000 — the largest ever imposed on a tribe — was ignored by the Mahsuds, the Commissioner of Dera Ismail Khan instituted a military blockade of their territory. Some of the money was paid but the outrages began again. After nearly a year of the blockade had failed to exact the full penalty, regular Indian troops were called in. By a series of surprise attacks from all corners of Mahsud country, they succeeded in inflicting heavy losses in men and cattle which forced the Mahsuds to come to terms and pay the fine in full; fourteen months after it had been first imposed, the blockade was lifted. A period of quiet followed, but in 1904 the Political Agent was murdered by a Mahsud sepoy of the South Waziristan Militia and it all began again. An Indian battalion was moved to Wana but the raiding and killing continued,

necessitating further reprisals. It was clear that, while the Mullah Powindah remained alive, South Waziristan would know no peace. His death in 1913 brought hope that tranquillity might now return, but the legacy he bequeathed to his people from his death-bed, urging them to carry on the struggle, ensured that this was not to be.

Elsewhere along the Frontier Curzon's claim was justified, but three years after he left India an expedition of divisional strength had to be mounted against the Zakha Khel Afridis under Major-General Willcocks, the commander of one of Kitchener's new formations, the 1st (Peshawar) Division. Smarting from their defeat in 1897, the Zakha Khel began raiding across the border from the Bazar Valley, culminating in the autumn of 1907 in a daring armed robbery in Peshawar itself. This was the first time a force had taken the field with the commander and staff with whom it had trained in peace, and the improvement in efficiency was remarkable. By using surprise and rapid movement, aided by greatly improved infantry training and the employment of a new 10-pounder mountain gun, Willcocks forced the Zakha Khel to submit within the space of a fortnight in February 1908. However, this uprising south of the Khyber sparked off trouble to the north among the Mohmands, who once again threatened Shabkadr Fort. Willcocks marched against them with despatch but, after routing them in late April, had to contend with a threat to Landi Kotal by tribesmen from across the political border. By a swift march down the Khyber and a successful attack, Willcocks overcame a dangerous situation which could have developed into war with Afghanistan. He then returned to complete his pacification of the Mohmands and by the end of May had brought his campaign to a very creditable conclusion.

A notable feature of these campaigns had been the increase in quality and quantity of the tribesmen's firearms. They had always been expert at stealing rifles from even the best-guarded garrisons, and their rifle-factories — notably that of the Adam Khel

A typical bungalow in the Peshawar cantonment.

Afridis near Kohat — had long been turning out replicas of Martinis and Lee-Metfords. By 1905 a whole new source of supply had been opened up by gun-running from Muscat on the Persian Gulf. By dhow across the Gulf, then by caravan across southern Persia, loads of rifles of all types and provenance — even a huge quantity of Martinis discarded by the Australian and New Zealand forces — began to reach the Frontier tribes. Not until 1909, when the Royal Navy sealed off Muscat with a blockade, did this great flood of weapons dwindle to a trickle. By then, however, there was scarcely a tribesman who did not own, at worst, a Martini, at best one of the new Lee-Enfields.

Curzon's solution of the Frontier problem was doubtless the best that could be devised at the time. Whatever benefits the new arrangement brought to the settled districts, it had little effect in the tribal territory. The tribes' deep-rooted independence, their traditional way of life could hardly be altered by a change of administration, however well-intentioned, and when these were exploited by influences hostile to the administrators, their volatile character was unlikely to remain immune.

12

A Quiet Summer

In 1908 Sir Harold Deane was succeeded as Chief Commissioner of the North-West Frontier Province by Sir George Roos-Keppel. Possessed of total self-confidence in his ability to govern, formidable in appearance and character, Roos-Keppel cared deeply for the Pathans and understood their every mood. Fluent in their language and idiom, he won their confidence and trust so that, throughout the difficult years of the Great War, he managed to keep most of the Frontier quiet. An important factor at this time was the attitude of the Amir Habibulla of Afghanistan. Despite his resentment at not having been consulted over the Anglo-Russian Convention of 1907, he nevertheless maintained his neutrality during the war, even when Turkey entered the conflict on Germany's side and the Sultan, the titular leader of Islam, called for a jehad against the Allies. He was unable to prevent a Turco-German mission arriving at Kabul, but by continual prevarication he managed to stall its requests for assistance against Britain. He made clear to tribal leaders his disapproval of any anti-British action without his authority, but pro-Turkish agents, working through certain mullahs, continued to do all they could to foment trouble among the tribes. The departure of much of the Indian Army for overseas, and news of British reverses at the hands of the Turks, strengthened their hand in some quarters, and in 1915 the Mohmands came out, followed by the Mahsuds. A blockade brought the Mohmands to heel but the Mahsuds, always mindful of the Mullah Powindah's last exhortations, could not be brought to terms until 1917. Notwithstand-

ing these outbreaks, the Frontier generally remained settled at a most testing time for Britain, and in January 1919 Roos-Keppel, who was about to hand over his responsibilities, felt able to report to the Viceroy, Lord Chelmsford, that 'everything on the frontier is so extraordinarily peaceful that it is safe to prophesy a quiet summer'.

With the Great War over, Habibulla now sought from the British Government some reward for the helpful attitude he had shown throughout, often at considerable risk to himself from the anti-British faction in his country. In particular, he looked for British recognition of the independence of his country where conduct of its foreign affairs was concerned, thereby hoping to terminate a situation which had existed since the Second Afghan War. His request for a seat at the Versailles Peace Conference had to be refused since attendance was confined to the belligerents, but Lord Chelmsford was not unsympathetic otherwise. However, before negotiations could begin, Habibulla was assassinated.

His brother, Nasrulla, assumed the title of Amir but found himself opposed by Habibulla's third son, Amanulla, who, with his hands on the treasury and arsenal of Kabul, and with the support of the army, proved the stronger contender for power. Nasrulla yielded, only to find himself arrested, tried for the murder of Habibulla and sentenced to life imprisonment. Amanulla, young, progressive and keen to modernise his country, was as set as his father on freeing Afghanistan from any foreign domination, a sentiment which commended itself to all sections of

Fort at Landi Kotal at the western end of the Khyber Pass.

New weapons of war on the Frontier. A 1914 Pattern Rolls-Royce armoured car on patrol, circa 1920. The major British armoured car effort was concentrated in India in the 1920s.

Afghan opinion, but his action against Nasrulla, the leader of more conservative elements, and his removal from office of others with similar leanings, rendered his position as Amir less than secure. By April 1919 it was apparent that, unless he could reconcile the conservatives with the progressives, he would be unlikely to survive.

Concurrent with the upsurge of nationalism in Afghanistan, a similar trend had arisen in India, culminating in riots and disorder in the Punjab. On 11 April troops under the command of Brigadier-General Dyer opened fire on a prohibited assembly at Amritsar, killing 379 people. This drastic action certainly had the salutary effect Dyer intended as far as quelling further disorder

was concerned, but it deeply shocked Indian public opinion.

Amanulla, scenting some advantage for himself in these disorders, the extent of which was misrepresented to him, was quick to condemn the British for their insensitivity and ingratitude to the Indians, who had loyally supported their cause in the war, and announced his belief in the justice of the Indian nationalists' actions. He also stated that, to ensure the disturbances did not spread over the border, he was moving troops up to the Durand Line.

It is uncertain whether Amanulla really intended to invade India or whether he merely wished to be ready to exploit any opportunity offered by the troubles in the Punjab, either by use of his regular forces or by inciting an uprising of the tribes. Either way, anti-British action on his part would serve to divert attention from the internal divisions of his own country and unite all factions behind him. Certainly a plan for invasion existed, for at this time the Afghan postmaster of Peshawar was busy concerting an insurrection to coincide with it. His rising was timed for 8 May but any surprise it might have achieved was forestalled by two events. First, the postmaster's designs and the Afghan invasion plan were reported to Roos-Keppel; second, Afghan troops crossed the border at the western end of the Khyber on 3 May and occupied the village of Bagh, the source of the water supply for Landi Kotal, then garrisoned by two companies of Indian infantry.

The Afghan regular army mustered some 50,000 men organised into 21 cavalry regiments and 75 infantry battalions with 280 modern guns. As a boost to this strength, it might expect additionally the services of up to 80,000 tribesmen. Against this, British forces in India totalled eight divisions, five independent brigades and three cavalry brigades, exclusive of the Frontier Militias, but the troops were no longer of the same calibre as they had been prior to 1914. The Indian Army had suffered grievously in overseas theatres during the war, many of its units were still abroad, demobilisation was in progress, and the ranks of many regiments were filled with little more than recruits. Of the former 61 British regular regiments in India, all save two cavalry and eight infantry had gone to war. Their place had been taken by units of the Territorial Force, part-time soldiers designed originally for home defence in the United Kingdom but who, on mobilisation in 1914, had volunteered for overseas service and been sent to India to release the regular regiments for service in France or the Near East. After four years garrison duty in

The railway through the Bolan Pass to Quetta and Chaman.

151

Tribesmen in the Kurram valley, 1919.

the 2nd Somerset Light Infantry was hurried through the Khyber in a convoy of 67 lorries with their canopies down to conceal their contents from unfriendly eyes in the pass. On the same day Roos-Keppel sealed off Peshawar with a cordon of troops and police and threatened to cut off the city's water supply unless the ringleaders of the plot were handed over. This had the desired effect and by dawn the next day Peshawar was secure.

Additional reinforcements were now sent forward up the Khyber, raising the troops at Landi Kotal to just over brigade strength, and on 9 May the Afghan positions at Bagh were attacked. The Third Afghan War had begun in earnest. Unfortunately, the brigadier in command detached nearly half his force to safeguard his north flank, and the attacking troops failed to capture all their objectives. Some of the prestige lost by this failure was retrieved by three BE2C aircraft of the Royal Air Force which made a spectacular bombing raid on a gathering of hostile tribesmen at Dacca, on the Afghan side of the border. Two days later Bagh was again attacked in greater strength. Covered by 18 guns and 22 machine-guns, the leading wave, 2nd North Staffords and two battalions of the 11th Gurkhas,* drove the Afghans from their positions with the bayonet, while the Royal Air Force harried their retreat back across the border.

In a letter to Chelmsford, Amanulla protested his innocence, still claiming his troops' advance had been purely precautionary, but Roos-Keppel, conscious of the need to ensure the Afghan defeat was not lost upon the tribes, insisted the pursuit be followed up across the border to Dacca. Once there, the badly-sited British camp came under long-range artillery fire, followed by an infantry assault. Though repulsed and a counter-attack put in next day, several set-backs delayed consolidation of the Dacca position and it was not until 17 May that the Afghans abandoned their defences and their guns.

Unfortunately, this success had the opposite effect to that anticipated and trouble broke out in the British rear along the line of

*A wartime regiment, raised in 1918, disbanded 1920.

India — a mundane task which had caused dissatisfaction from the beginning — all they were interested in was a swift return to civilian life; certainly they were in no mood for a campaign on the Frontier. Only by a direct appeal from the Commander-in-Chief was a possible refusal to obey orders averted. On the other hand, as a counter-balance to any deficiencies in manpower or morale, the British forces enjoyed a much greater superiority in *matériel*: more machine-guns, wireless communications, armoured cars, motor transport and, above all, the newest service, the Royal Air Force.

Although the Afghan intentions, following the incursion of 3 May, were not fully evident, Roos-Keppel urged upon Chelmsford the necessity of ejecting them from Bagh before they could incite the tribes to rise in support. The garrison at Landi Kotal urgently required reinforcing but the potential trouble in Peshawar also had to be nipped in the bud. Only one battalion could be spared immediately for the first task, and on 7 May

Interior of the fort at Wana, Waziristan.

The type of men enlisted into the South Waziristan Militia. Photograph taken after the 1919 troubles when it had been reconstituted as the South Waziristan Scouts.

communication through the Khyber Pass which was guarded by the Khyber Rifles. This force, despite its failure in 1897, had displayed total loyalty during the Afridi troubles of 1908, but now began to show severe signs of disaffection with many desertions from the ranks. Faced with a complete breakdown of discipline, Roos-Keppel had no choice but to disarm those that remained and disband the force. Further deterioration of the internal security situation in and around Peshawar followed and numbers of troops had to be diverted to contain it. Chelmsford decided that all this could best be countered by a drive against the source of disaffection — Afghanistan itself — and consequently ordered a continuation of the advance from Dacca to Jalalabad. Before this could get under way, ominous news came from the south.

In support of the Khyber attack, the Afghan plan had envisaged two other advances, one in the Kurram, the second against Quetta. At the latter the British commander decided to strike first, and on 27 May he attacked and captured the Afghan fortress of Spin Baldak. This stabilised affairs in the south, but the centre was different matter. Here in Khost, west of the Kurram Valley, General Nadir Khan, the most capable of the Afghan commanders, disposed of 14 battalions. His intentions were unknown to the local British commander, Brigadier-General Eustace, but since Thal, at the south end of

The arrival of the Afghan delegates at Landi Khana at the close of the Third Afghan War, 1919. Note the double line of white stones in the foreground and running up the hill in the left background marking the political border or Durand Line.

154

the Kurram Valley, seemed a likely objective its garrison was reinforced to a strength of four battalions. Eustace was also concerned that Nadir Khan might strike at the upper Tochi Valley further south, held only by the North Waziristan Militia who could not be relied upon without the support of regular troops; these Eustace did not have. Accordingly he ordered the evacuation of the militia posts. As they withdrew, the Tochi Wazirs rose in arms and the Wazir and Afridi elements of the Militia either deserted or proved unreliable. Disaffection spread to the South Waziristan Militia around Wana, where mutinous sepoys seized the treasury and a quantity of ammunition. Major Russell, the commandant, had to fight his way southwards with a handful of loyal militiamen across appalling country, in intense heat and harassed constantly by tribesmen and renegade sepoys, until a relief column of the Zhob Militia was encountered. Notwithstanding Russell's fine achievement in trying to save something of his command, the South Waziristan Militia ceased to exist as a fighting force until reconstituted two years later. Its northern counterpart remained in being, though with diminished numbers.

A Mahsud tribesman, about 1920.

A Royal Artillery mountain battery, 1920, with British gunners in front, Indian muleteers and gun-mules behind.

155

A picquet of the North-West Frontier Constabulary, formerly the Border Military Police, guarding the progress of a column.

2nd Battalion 5th Gurkha Rifles (Frontier Force) in action against the Mahsuds at Ahnai Tangi, 14 January 1920. Painting by Fred Roe.

Still, the unreliability of these two forces, together with that of the Khyber Rifles, was a severe blow to the system of entrusting security in the border areas to local levies, and the whole of Waziristan was now given over to lawlessness.

Action to restore order therein had to wait, for meanwhile Nadir Khan had advanced to besiege Thal on 27 May. Eustace was outnumbered and outgunned by the enemy, many of his troops, all Indian, were young and inexperienced, and supplies were short; it was uncertain how long he could hold out. At Peshawar, a fresh division then arriving from Lahore for the advance on Jalalabad was diverted to Kurram. Part of it was sent to hold Kohat, which was undefended, while Dyer's brigade was ordered to make all speed to relieve Thal. Dyer was ill, tired and under a cloud from the Amritsar affair; the quality of his troops was mixed and his only British battalion consisted of disgruntled Territorials of the 1st/25th London Regiment. He may have been anathema to politicians but he had a way with soldiers, and when he appealed to the ill-assorted men of his command for a supreme effort to save Thal, all of them, Punjabis, Dogras, Gurkhas and Londoners, responded with a will. Short of food and water, with little rest since leaving Peshawar, and marching under a blistering sun, they covered the last eighteen miles towards the besieged garrison in twelve hours. Finding the approaches to Thal barred by tribesmen to north and south, Dyer opened fire with his guns on both contingents simultaneously, then launched his infantry against the southern flank. Hammered by the artillery, the tribes would not await the infantry attack and by the afternoon the way to Thal was opened.

The next day, 2 June, Dyer moved against the Afghan regulars to the west, but before the attack could develop, an envoy from Nadir Khan came forward under a flag of truce to request a cease-fire. Unknown to Dyer, the Amir had asked for an armistice on 31 May but this had not yet been granted. With his men in action, and unwilling to take chances, Dyer gave the envoy an uncompromising answer: 'My guns will give an immediate reply, and a further reply will be sent by the Divisional Commander to whom the letter has been forwarded.' With this, he ordered the resumption of the attack. Before the infantry could close, however, the Afghans hurriedly withdrew westwards, pursued by cavalry, armoured cars and aircraft. On 3 June an armistice was signed and hostilities ceased. By his leadership, determination and sound handling of his guns and infantry, Dyer, though beset by personal problems, had saved Thal and possibly the Frontier. But it availed his career nothing, for shortly afterwards, when called to account for the severity of his action at Amritsar — which he believed had saved the Punjab from bloody insurrection — he was relieved of his command and died not long afterwards.

Although Afghan regular forces had been driven from British territory and Afghan cities had felt the weight of the Royal Air Force's bombers, the Amir's delegates approached the peace conference assembled at Rawalpindi in July in less than conciliatory mood. The negotiations were acrimonious, but in the end a treaty was signed on 8 August, the most important clause of which gave the Afghans what they most wanted, and could probably have gained without a war — the right to conduct their own foreign affairs as a fully independent state. The Durand Line was reaffirmed as the political boundary and the Afghans undertook not to intrigue with the tribes on the British side.

The Third Afghan War might have been over but the unrest it had stirred up, notably in Waziristan, grew worse and worse. Always ready to exploit weakness, as the withdrawal of the Militias had been so interpreted, Mahsuds and Wazirs found a common unity in disorder and tumult. Well armed with looted rifles and ammunition and with their ranks swollen by militia deserters, whose military training gave useful expertise and intelligence to the tribal lashkars, they embarked on a bitter campaign of resistance to authority which, with a few short respites, was to continue virtually up to the outbreak of World War Two in 1939.

The first attempt to subdue them began in November 1919 with Major-General Skeen's operations against the Tochi Wazirs. These achieved success fairly rapidly but, when Skeen turned on the Mahsuds in early December, his troops, all Indian save for some British gunners, found themselves pitted against implacable opponents who fought with gallantry and skill. Some of his battalions were second-line units raised in wartime, others had a disproportionately high number of young soldiers with inexperienced officers. When put to the test, some of these battalions failed and had to be replaced. But against such failures must be set other instances: like the heroic fighting withdrawal to evacuate their wounded by the 34th Sikh Pioneers, after being abandoned by their covering troops when constructing a picquet on a feature known as Black Hill; or the stubborn fight in support of the 2nd/5th Gurkhas during the eight-day battle in January 1920 at Ahnai Tangi by some very green young sepoys, whom an eyewitness called 'those children of the 2nd/76th Punjabis'; or the gallant counter-attack against a mass of Mahsuds by ten men of the 4th/39th Garhwal Rifles led by Lieutenant Kenny, who was awarded a posthumous Victoria Cross. In the fighting at Ahnai Tangi the Mahsuds lost heavily and it was these casualties, coupled with the destruction of their villages a month later, that broke their will to fight — at least for a while. As the Mahsuds licked their wounds, it was the turn of the Wana Wazirs. When attacked in November 1920, they appealed to the Mahsuds for help, but with none forthcoming, the Wazir opposition crumbled and on 22 December Wana itself was re-occupied.

Minor forays and raids continued throughout 1921, but a major change of policy was now in the offing. Henceforth, it was decided, if Waziristan was to be kept quiet, a permanent garrison of regular troops would have to be maintained there in much closer support to the reconstituted Militia. The place chosen was in the very heart of the territory, at Razmak.

A Bristol F2B Mk II of No 20 Squadron, RAF, flying at 1,000 feet over the Khyber Pass at 1030 hours on 9 December 1925. Bristol Fighters gave invaluable service as General Purpose aircraft in India with Nos 5, 20, 27, 28 and 31 Squadrons during the 1920s, the last being withdrawn in 1932, replaced by Wapitis. Note the message pick-up hook for Army co-operation duties.

DH9A aircraft of No 60 Squadron, Royal Air Force flying over Frontier terrain in the late 1920s. The RAF made a significant contribution to Frontier operations from the Third Afghan War onwards.

RAF groundcrew cautiously attempting to start a DH9A's engine during the wet season in India. The weather on the North West Frontier could be a great hindrance to RAF operations. The RAF's standard day bomber during the 1920s, the DH9A, known familiarly as the Ninak, equipped Nos 27 and 60 Squadrons in India as a General Purpose type from 1919 until superseded by the Westland Wapiti in 1929.

A Westland Wapiti of No 60 Squadron, RAF, bombing on the North-Western Frontier. The Wapiti, the RAF's major General Purpose type of the early 1930s, served with eight squadrons in India. Combining several roles, General Purpose aircraft were ideal for 'control without occupation'.

Vickers Victorias of No 70 Squadron, RAF, normally based in Iraq, photographed in January 1929 at Peshawar. Eight of its Victorias with a few from the Indian Bomber Transport Flight, and DH9As, carried out the 1928–1929 evacuation of Kabul. This was the first major air-lift.

A Hawker Hart of No 39 Squadron, No 2 Indian Wing, RAF photographed over Gilgit. The Hart two-seat day bomber served with Nos 11, 39 and 60 Squadrons, RAF, in India from 1931, replacing their Westland Wapitis, until superseded by Bristol Blenheims in 1938–1939. An Army co-operation variant, the Audax, replaced the Wapitis of Nos 20 and 27 Squadrons, RAF, in India in 1931.

13

Red Shirts and the Fakir

The decision to establish a permanent presence of regular troops in Waziristan from 1923 found little favour with the then Chief Commissioner of the North-West Frontier Province, Sir John Maffey. Apart from not being consulted about it, he held the view that such garrisons would be a constant affront to the fanatical independence of the tribes, and that the extended, highly vulnerable lines of communication of the garrisons would not only invite attack and ambush, but would diminish the ability of the troops to dominate the territory. He urged that tribal disorder should be discouraged by the seizure of hostages whose release could only be effected by the submission of offenders, and that the quick and efficient reaction of troops stationed outside tribal territory should be speeded up by the improvement of communications to permit the use of motor transport and enhanced by the employment of aircraft. However, by the time he voiced his objections, the decision was irrevocable.

Razmak itself contained a brigade of six battalions, including one British, a mountain artillery brigade, and all the necessary ancillary services, housed in brick or wooden buildings surrounded by a strong perimeter wall with machine-gun posts sited along it, and protected by a barbed wire fence and a ring of permanent picquets farther out. In time, it became just like any other Indian cantonment except that the troops were on an active service footing and no women were allowed. To the north, along the line of the Tochi river back to Bannu, were another seven battalions, while to the south, between Tank and Jandola, was another brigade. The

Waziristan militias were reconstituted as the Tochi Scouts and the South Waziristan Scouts. Over the next dozen years the quartering of the territory by columns from the new garrisons, the increasing confidence of the Scouts, and the new dimension of control afforded by the air arm, all helped to damp down the lawlessness of Mahsuds and Wazirs. But it was all preventative, rather than curative, and as time went by, Maffey's forebodings would prove to be justified.

Before that occurred, the chief scene of trouble moved away from Waziristan, back up north to Peshawar itself. The Government of India Act of 1919 had initiated certain reforms with the aim of associating Indians with every branch of Indian administration and the gradual development of self-governing institutions — the so-called dyarchic experiment. These reforms were not extended to the North-West Frontier Province on the advice of Roos-Keppel, who considered the Pathans were not yet ready for them. His view was not shared by at least one Pathan, a political agitator with a powerful personality and much influence over the poor: Abdul Ghaffar Khan, who had been politically active since 1919, and who now began to arouse the Pathans of the Province over this discrimination against them. In 1920 he joined the Congress Party of Gandhi and Nehru which, though primarily Hindu and non-violent and thus in complete contrast to his own religion and sentiments, he saw as an increasingly powerful anti-British instrument. Nine years later he formed his own organisation, unarmed but paramilitary in style and with a rudimentary

Razmak Camp, Waziristan, in 1923, showing tented accommodation and the foundations for the later permanent buildings.

uniform of shirts dyed with brick-dust, which gave rise to its colloquial name of the 'Red Shirts'. Although these militant young Pathans drilled openly, and Abdul Ghaffar Khan and his agents preached sedition and violence along the Frontier from Bannu to Malakand, the authorities took no action against him, either underestimating the strength of the movement, or believing that if it was ignored it might wither of its own accord. However, it did not wither, and Abdul Ghaffar Khan's prestige grew, his organisation prospered and governmental inactivity was interpreted as incapacity and therefore weakness.

Eventually, during a huge Red Shirt rally at Peshawar in late April 1930, the performance of an openly seditious melodrama calculated to incite anti-Government hatred convinced the authorities they must arrest Abdul Ghaffar Khan and other Red Shirt and Congress leaders present. Despite the explosive potential of arresting them at such a time and place, inadequate security precautions

were taken. Savage rioting ensued, which the police were unable to contain, and the military had to be called in. The mob grew more and more frenzied, armoured cars were set alight with petrol, and the Royal Garhwal Rifles had to open fire to avoid being overwhelmed. Gradually, the troops gained the upper hand and order was restored. Then, at the request of the city elders, the military were withdrawn and the rioting broke out afresh. After eight days anarchy the army was ordered back into the city and took over control.

Although Peshawar was quiet by the end of May, the troubles had stirred up the Afridis, may of whom had been in the city during the riots. At a tribal jirga on 2 May the elders had counselled forbearance but the young hotheads were all for action. A lashkar was formed south-west of Peshawar and in June advanced on the city. It was dispersed by columns of cavalry and aircraft, but reformed and continued to raid over the Peshawar district throughout August. It was then

163

Tribesman in Waziristan of the type that gave so much trouble in the 1920s and 1930s. The clothing has not changed much in a century but the Lee-Enfield has replaced the jezail.

decided that the area from which the dissidents had been operating could only be controlled by the establishment of permanent outposts interlinked by motorable roads. This required a strong division of troops, supported by aircraft, to accomplish and it was not until October 1931 that a settlement was finally made with the Afridis.

By that time Abdul Ghaffar Khan, having been released from prison in March, was again active with his Red Shirts in the Peshawar Valley. His anti-British speeches grew more venomous and a formal alliance was contracted between his organisation and the Congress Party, though relations between the two were uneven. His agitation was tolerated for a while by the authorities, but when he began to interfere in civil affairs they had had enough, declaring the Red Shirts an illegal organisation and arresting him and four of his henchmen, before dispersing them to prisons in different parts of India. Nevertheless, his struggle had not been without results. In 1932 the status of the Province was raised from a Chief Commissionership to a Governorship, and its political rights and institutions became the same as in the rest of India, with a Pathan, Sahibzada Abdul Qayyum, as chief minister; in 1937 it shared with all other provinces the further advance towards self-government specified by the 1935 Government of India Act. On Abdul Qayyum's death his post went to Abdul Ghaffar Khan's elder brother, Dr Khan Sahib, who was also a strong supporter of the Congress.

In view of the inflammatory effect of the Red Shirt troubles on the Afridis, it would have been remarkable if their neighbours to the north, the Mohmands, had not been similarly affected. The upper Mohmands had given trouble in 1927 when, stirred up by two religious firebrands, a lashkar had descended on the lower clans, whose maliks had maintained a friendly attitude towards the Government; in doing so it crossed the administrative border and fired on British troops but was quickly dispersed by the Royal Air Force. In 1933 the upper Mohmands came out again in a belated

The Peshawar riots of 1930. Indian Pattern Crossley armoured cars of the Royal Tank Corps, British infantry and the Royal Garhwal Rifles deployed in the streets. Armoured cars were often called upon to quell riots. By 1930 all the R.T.C.'s armoured cars were in India, the majority on the Frontier, while those on the plains were responsible for internal security.

demonstration of solidarity with the Red Shirts. An expedition advanced up the Gandab Valley to punish them and build a road through it in case further operations became necessary to protect the lower clans, but the road sowed the seeds of renewed trouble in 1935 when the Mohmands started to destroy it. Air action having failed to subdue the lashkar, a force of three brigades had to be committed, two of which were commanded by officers who were to achieve high rank and renown in World War Two, the future Field Marshals Sir Claude Auchinleck and Viscount Alexander.

In the final attack of this campaign the strength of the enemy opposition was seriously underestimated, and the Guides Infantry, since 1922 re-designated 5th Battalion of the 12th Frontier Force Regiment,* found itself attacking the enemy's strongest position out of supporting range from the rest of its brigade. The ground was difficult in the extreme, offering every advantage to the defenders, and the need to occupy intervening ridges to give covering fire left only two weak platoons for the final assault up a

*In the 1922 re-organisation, existing regiments became battalions of larger regiments.

Machine-gunners of the 4th Battalion 15th Punjabis during operations near Ladha in Waziristan 1933.

Lorry convoy on the road built by the Peshawar Brigade over the Nahakhi Pass in Mohmand country, 1935.

Political officer announcing terms at a jirga, 1935.

In trouble! Light Tank Mark II, the type used in the Mohmand operations of 1935 by the 2nd Light Tank Company, the first operational use of tanks since 1918.

knife-edge enfiladed from both flanks. Communication with the artillery failed and the company commander was killed. The Adjutant, Captain Meynell, went forward to take over and, being joined by four more platoons, inflicted heavy casualties on the Mohmands before his position was encircled and overrun. Of the 138 men with him, only 31 got clear unscathed. The battalion commander, Major Good, himself wounded, ordered a withdrawal and eventually fire was brought down on the abandoned position by artillery and light tanks. Despite the failure to hold the mountain, the casualties suffered by the tribesmen in this battle drove the Mohmands to seek terms. Meynell was subsequently awarded a posthumous Victoria Cross for his gallant and determined leadership.*

Despite the increased firepower provided by tanks, armoured cars and aircraft, these punitive expeditions were essentially still as they had always been — expensive, time-consuming and lacking the element of surprise. In the twenties, with the independence of the Royal Air Force threatened by cuts in defence expenditure, the Chief of the Air

* The last to be granted for Frontier operations.

Staff, Sir Hugh, later Lord Trenchard, proposed the novel idea that areas of difficult terrain peopled by unruly tribesmen could be more effectively controlled by air power alone. The RAF had proved its worth in the Third Afghan War, but then it had been acting in support of ground forces. Trenchard's proposal, 'air control' as it was called, envisaged a reversal of these roles. If summonses to surrender were ignored, punitive action against centres of unrest would, after due warnings to evacuate women and children, be taken by the air arm alone with bombing attacks on the villages and surrounding areas concerned, followed by an 'air blockade' to keep tribesmen away from their homes and crops and generally disrupt their way of life until hardship and inconvenience forced the dissidents to submit. Only after submission had been made would troops or constabulary be used to ensure order was maintained on the ground.

Trenchard's plan proved highly successful in Iraq, then under British mandate, as well as in Aden and Trans-Jordan, all three territories being placed under air control. However, on the North-West Frontier where, unlike the other territories, the Army was in strength and jealous of its preserves, the theory of air control was never fully tried out. Furthermore, the Government of India was unwilling to allocate adequate resources from its defence budget to the Royal Air Force, with the result that aircraft serviceability suffered, enabling the Army to claim that climatic and geographic conditions of the area were unsuited to purely aerial policing. Operations on the Frontier therefore remained under Army control with the RAF in a supporting role. In 1937 it was to be eventually agreed that in the event of trouble with Afghanistan, or a major tribal uprising, the offensive would be taken from the air while ground forces remained on the defensive. However, the situation never arose and even if it had the RAF would have found itself still hampered by lack of funds.

Nevertheless, aircraft did much useful work in support of ground operations and, in the late twenties, the RAF performed an important task which could hardly have been undertaken by the Army without precipitat-

ing a fourth Afghan war. By the end of 1928 the attempts by Amanulla to modernise his country had driven many of his subjects into open revolt and fighting broke out in Kabul. The British Legation found itself under fire from both sides and the Envoy, Sir Francis Humphreys, requested an airlift from India to evacuate the several hundred British and other foreigners from Afghanistan. The only aircraft available in India were the DH9As of Nos 27 and 60 Squadrons, together with a few Bristol F2B Fighters and a couple of new Westland Wapitis, then undergoing tropical trials. The Air Officer Commanding, Air-Vice-Marshal Sir Geoffrey Salmond, accordingly ordered the DH9As to be stripped of all war equipment, at the same time requesting the services of No 70 Squadron from Iraq which was equipped with proper transport aircraft, the Vickers Victoria.

After a DH9A managed to land under fire at Kabul to establish wireless communications, the evacuation of women and children began on 23 December and was successfully

South Waziristan Scouts on parade at Sararogha fort.

Men of the 2nd Battalion Border Regiment on the march on the Frontier in the 1930s. Pith topees were now worn in the field instead of Wolseley helmets.

accomplished in a week. With the fighting continuing, Humphreys closed the Legation and the evacuation went on. By 25 February 1929 Squadron Leader Maxwell of No 70 Squadron and his pilots had brought the last of 586 people and 41 tons of baggage to safety in India, having completed 84 flights across the mountains in one of the worst winters ever experienced on the Frontier. For the crews in their open cockpits flying in temperatures as low as minus 20 degrees centigrade, this had been a considerable ordeal, yet, although several aircraft suffered damage, not a single casualty was sustained throughout this first major airlift of the Royal Air Force.

While the evacuation was still in progress Amanulla was forced to concede defeat and abdicated. Soviet Russia, as eager as the Tsars had been to have a finger in the Afghan pie, had, with Amanulla's connivance, been infiltrating agents into the country and on his fall made an abortive attempt to save him. A confused period followed, but then Nadir Khan, the attacker of Thal in 1919, seized power in Kabul and was proclaimed king as Nadir Shah. He ruled wisely and firmly for four years and, being of conservative inclinations, had no truck with any Soviet interference, but in 1933, after executing a man who, with Soviet backing, had plotted to restore Amanulla, he was assassinated. Since his heir was under age, his two brothers ruled as co-regents and, with an effective Prime Minister, maintained good relations with India over Frontier affairs. Nevertheless, such cordiality did not prevent the arrival in 1935 of some so-called 'technicians' from Nazi Germany, who doubtless had a more sinister role in addition to the construction work they undertook, nor the appearance in 1938 of other pro-Hitler emissaries, among them the ex-Mufti of Jerusalem, long a thorn in the British side in the Near East. Baulked of a hand in Afghan affairs, the Soviets found more fruitful soil for their anti-British seeds,

An Indian Pattern Crossley armoured car of the 3rd Royal Tank Corps in Waziristan, 1936. From 1931 armoured car companies converted into light tank companies, the light tank being much more effective on the Frontier. The Corps left India in 1938, after supervising the mechanization of the Indian Army.

in the person and activities of one who was to loom large in the minds of Frontier soldiers and officials in the late thirties — a Tori Khel Wazir named Mirza Ali Khan, better known as the Fakir of Ipi.

Until 1936 he had devoted himself entirely to the religious life, but in April of that year there occurred at Bannu the trial of a Moslem student on a charge of abducting a Hindu girl, whom it was alleged had subsequently been converted to Islam. A crowd of angry Moslems, stirred up by agitators, delayed the trial and had to be dispersed. Among its leaders was the Fakir of Ipi who, claiming that the incident was but one example of growing government interference in religious matters, soon began to attract a large following among the tribal hotheads. There were many already ripe for armed re-assertion of their independence in the face of what appeared to them as the weakening will of the British to govern: an impression derived from the constitutional changes in India and one which agents of the Congress did everything to foster. With the Fakir's anti-British message spreading apace, the

authorities ordered the Tori Khel maliks either to silence or expel him. This they claimed they could not do without British support but that, even if such support was forthcoming, it might be opposed.

In late November 1936 it was decided to demonstrate the Government's right, agreed with the Tori Khel in 1935, to move troops through the Khaisora Valley by marching a column from Razmak eastwards, to join up at the village of Bichhe Kashkai with another from the Bannu Brigade advancing southwards from Mir Ali. The demonstration was to be a peaceful one and no offensive action was to be taken unless troops were attacked. The Razmak column, or Razcol, formed of the 1st Northamptonshire Regiment, 5th/12th Frontier Force Regiment(Guides), 6th/13th Frontier Force Rifles, 1st/9th Gurkhas and three mountain batteries, began the march without incident, but on the third day, some ten miles from Bichhe Kashkai, came under fire in a narrow valley. The column pressed on under cover of its picquets but the resistance increased and the rearguard did not reach camp until after dark. Meanwhile,

170

the two Indian battalions from Mir Ali, or Tocol, had met even stiffer opposition and were unable to reach the rendezvous until the following day. Since rations and ammunition were short, and the combined casualties of both columns totalled more than a hundred, all the troops were withdrawn to Mir Ali, the rearguard being hotly pressed. Instead of demonstrating a show of strength and invincibility, the operation, due to the limitations imposed on it, had had to surrender the initiative to the enemy, whose numbers rapidly grew from 500 to about 2,000 as a result, and consequently had slowed down and sustained quite heavy losses. In the tribesmen's eyes Government prestige fell and the Fakir of Ipi's rose proportionately.

The rules governing punitive expeditions had changed considerably since the nineteenth century. Although the troops' armoury was greatly enhanced, with tanks, armoured cars, automatic weapons and air-

craft, political considerations now required that, as John Masters, the novelist and officer of the 4th Gurkhas in this campaign, put it: 'We fought with one hand behind our backs.' Any troubled region was bounded by carefully laid down limits and known as the 'proscribed area'. Outside it troops could take no action at all until shot at; inside it they might not fire at any group of less than ten men unless they were armed and off a path. The problem of spotting where the paths lay and the ease with which tribesmen could conceal weapons made the swift reaction troops needed if they were to survive doubly difficult to achieve. Any surprise that aircraft might have been able to attain was hopelessly circumscribed by the high-level authority that had to be obtained first, followed by the dropping of leaflets informing the tribesmen of the target to be attacked. Every military rule for effective Frontier warfare was in conflict with political rules — all of which

Men of 1st Battalion Northamptonshire Regiment halting while on column from Razmak during operations against the Fakir of Ipi, 1936. Compare the dress with that worn by the same battalion in the Tirah, page 133.

the tribesmen knew very well and took every advantage. When troops saw the tortured, castrated and flayed corpses of any of their comrades unfortunate enough to fall into Pathan hands, it was difficult to stomach the constant political prohibitions on military freedom of action. Although the British rules had changed, the Pathans' had not; as in Kipling's day, the women still came out 'to cut up the remains'.

For the next twelve months, after the attack in the Khaisora Valley, the Fakir of Ipi kept the flame of insurrection alight all over Waziristan. No sooner was one outbreak dealt with than fresh trouble would erupt somewhere else, Wazirs, Mahsuds, Bhittanis, even Afghans from across the border rallying to his summons. By April 1937 four extra brigades had been brought in from India to reinforce the garrisons of Razmak, Bannu and Wana. The aim of the army commander, General Coleridge, was to force the enemy to stand and fight so that a decisive defeat could be inflicted, but the Fakir was far too wily to be caught in this way and, since he almost always retained the initiative, the army generally had to respond to his moves.

Nevertheless, the enemy did not have everything their own way, as was seen in May when two brigades advanced against the heart of hostile activity on the Sham plain, the watershed between the Khaisora and Shaktu valleys, prior to striking at Arsal Kot, a village where the Fakir had long had a stronghold. As one brigade prepared to advance frontally against the high ground held by 4,000 tribesmen, the Bannu Brigade, led by the Tochi Scouts, made a daring and hazardous night march up the Iblanke spur to the east. It was pitch dark and the going extremely difficult, but by dawn the troops were in position across the enemy's right flank and rear. The mountain battery and machine-guns opened fire, the Scouts and 2nd/11th Sikhs went forward supported by the 4th Gurkhas, while at the same time the other brigade began its ascent to the crest from the Khaisora. Taken completely by surprise and demoralised by this attack from a direction in which they felt themselves secure, the tribesmen rapidly melted away. Arsal Kot was subsequently destroyed, though needless to say the Fakir had gone by the time the troops reached it. Could he have been taken the insurrection would have collapsed, but all attempts to seize him proved fruitless.

For much of the time troops were occupied with the construction or improvement of

Machine-gunners of the 3rd Gurkha Rifles paraded with their mules, 1936.

A night-picquet of 1st Battalion Northamptonshire Regiment manning a sangar in Waziristan, 1936. The soldiers have exchanged their topees for cap comforters during the night.

roads to open up the country so as to permit more rapid deployment, or the re-opening of existing roads which had been cut. All road movement was highly susceptible to attack as, for example, the ambush of a convoy to Wana in the Shahur Tangi defile in April, during which seven officers and 45 men were killed and 47 more wounded, the whole gorge being blocked by blazing vehicles. The tribesmen well knew that the roads threatened the inaccessibility of their mountain hide-outs and that they also offered tempting pickings. Therefore the passage of all convoys and columns had to be protected by temporary or permanent picquets along the route, the establishment of which frequently involved troops in considerable skirmishing, sometimes quite heavy fighting. On one occasion a platoon picquet of the resident British battalion at Razmak, the 1st Northamptons, had to hold its position under continuous fire for seven hours, an action for which one Distinguished Conduct Medal and two Military Medals were subsequently awarded.

Vickers machine-gun of 3rd Battalion 11th Sikh Regiment in action in Waziristan 1936.

A typical day of an infantry battalion on column in Waziristan was described by a member of the same battalion: 'At 5 a.m. a Gunner trumpeter sounds the four Gs for Reveille. Breakfast is ready about five o'clock. Soon the column moves on its way. First go the picquetting troops; half doubling, half shuffling, they push out ahead as rapidly as possible. Every hill or commanding feature from which the Pathans can threaten the progress of the column is garrisoned by anything from a platoon to a company, depending on the size of the feature. It is not merely a matter of running up a hill and sitting there, because the hill may already be held, so every picquet going up is covered by machine-guns and mountain guns, so that at the slightest sign of opposition fire can be brought down immediately. As can well be imagined it is a slow business. Some of the hills are, perhaps, 1,000 feet above the track, and the going is difficult and precipitous. It may be forty minutes before the picquetting troops reach the top and the column cannot move forward until they are in position.'

Each picquet had to remain in position until signalled to withdraw by the rearguard commander, who had to ensure none were missed. On regaining the column the picquet would be sent forward to rejoin its battalion and was then available for further picquets. If opposition was met, the whole advance ground to a halt while the position was attacked — though the tribesmen seldom awaited the final assault. On reaching the evening's camp site: 'We march in at attention, arms sloped as neat and smart as we can be, and line up in our allotted portion of the perimeter. Arms are piled, equipment and boots taken off and *chaplies* (sandals) carried in one's pack are put on. Tools are issued and then the work of making the perimeter wall and digging commences; no food or rest until that is done.'

After marching and picquetting all day, the building of the stone wall was tiring work. Machine-gun posts were sited, the mountain guns ranged on likely targets, while some platoons had to go out to construct sangars, surrounded by barbed wire, on commanding heights to protect the camp. At 5 p.m. the men had their dinners and dug their sleeping pits. Lights out sounded at 9.30, when all was quiet: 'Although some 2,000 souls are down to a well-earned rest, there is no lack of vigil or alertness along the perimeter walls; double sentries are patrolling, men are awake alongside the guns . . . the orderly officers quietly go their rounds. Suddenly the stillness of the night is broken by 'crack-thump' from the high ground overlooking the camp. The wily Pathan snipers have started their nightly task. Firing goes on for some time and no action is taken from inside the camp, until suddenly a burst of machine-gun fire rings out. The gunner on duty has spotted a sniper's flash and is spraying the area. A

Gurkhas building a sangar, 1937.

174

Verey light goes up from one of the picquets and all is silent again. Later it starts again from elsewhere and goes on intermittently all night. All too soon morning comes and the column is again on its way.'

By dint of quartering the troubled areas in this way, by destroying hostile villages either with air or ground action, the army made its presence felt but, with the Fakir still at large, nothing very conclusive was achieved. Nevertheless, by December 1937, many of the rebels were growing weary of the bombing and fighting and the Fakir's influence was finding a less ready response. It was then felt that the presence of so many troops was counter-productive: the more there were deployed, the greater the number of tribesmen prepared to resist. Consequently, it was decided to withdraw most of the additional troops, leaving only the former garrisons, in the hope that this might have a pacifying effect.

Trouble flared up again in 1938–39, though on a reduced scale, despite a daring attack by a lashkar on the town of Bannu, which was only driven off after heavy fighting; a raid injurious to British prestige and elevating to the Fakir's. He was never captured and continued to do his utmost to stir up trouble, but by and large Waziristan, and the Frontier as a whole, quietened down and was to remain so for the next eight years.

This was just as well, for from 1939 onwards larger and more pressing tasks claimed the attention of the British and Indian Armies. The basic military attributes that so many had learned on the Frontier hills were to stand them in good stead against Germans and Italians in East Africa, the Western Desert and Italy. Yet it was in none of those theatres that the Army in India was to fight its greatest campaign. For years that army had looked to the mountain ranges and high passes of the North-West; that was where the threat to India lay, out of Central Asia, that was the task for which they had trained, that was the region that had to be kept stable and secure by watch and ward and countless expeditions. It was the way the invader had always come, back over the centuries. For nigh on a hundred years the British soldier, Indian sepoy and Gurkha rifleman had waited to defend India against Afghans, Persians or Russians. But Skobolev's Mongol horde had never galloped over the Malakand, the Amir's infantry had never paraded through Peshawar and no Cossacks had ever clattered through Quetta; except briefly in 1919, no invader had come. When he did, it was not through the Khyber or the Bolan, but out of the jungles of Assam and Manipur, on the frontier to which no-one had given a second thought — the North-East. In 1944 the legions of Japan hurled themselves against Kohima and Imphal, and the modern counterparts of those who for so long had guarded the North-West fought savagely to save the North-East. As all the world knows their efforts were finally crowned with victory, and the warriors of the Emperor of Japan were hurled back whence they came; a fate, one would like to think, that would have befallen the armies of the Tsar, had they ever marched out of Asia.

Epilogue:
Changing the Guard

In 1947, two years after the Japanese surrender and the end of the Second World War, British rule in India was finally terminated with the partition of the sub-continent into a Moslem Pakistan and a Hindu India, both fully independent states. In the North-West Frontier Province the British civil and military authorities handed over their responsibilities to those of Pakistan. The Province escaped relatively lightly from the communal violence and bloodshed in 1948 that had accompanied Partition, but its incorporation into Pakistan had not been without problems before Independence Day.

Before World War Two many Pathans had seen the Congress Party as their best allies against the British. After it, although Dr Khan Sahib and his Congress supporters had defeated Jinnah's Moslem League at the Provincial elections, the prospect of a Hindu-dominated Congress began to sway public opinion in favour of the Moslem League, who were demanding a separate state, Pakistan. Nehru underestimated support for the latter, and the hostility with which he was received in the Province by Pathans during his efforts to bolster Dr Khan came as a shock to him. The latter, still in office, tried to clamp down on the Moslem League but disorder broke out, riots and inter-communal fighting spread throughout the province and troops had to be called in. In April 1947 the Viceroy, Lord Mountbatten, toured the Province and announced that a referendum would be held to decide whether it should go to Pakistan or India. The Khan brothers tried to rally support for a separate Pathan state,

Pakhtunistan, but this impractical notion gained no ground. The Province, including all the tribes between the administrative border and the Durand Line, threw in their lot with Pakistan with a vote ratio of a hundred to one.

Before the referendum took place, the Afghan Government lodged a claim that, following the British withdrawal, the whole Pathan country as far as the Indus should revert to Afghanistan. Subsequently, this claim was tempered to a demand for the creation of a separate Pathan state, similar to the Khan brothers' proposal, but, since in the Afghan view the international frontier of the Durand Line had become ineffective after the British departure, such a state would simply merge into Afghanistan. Pakistan took the line that, in international law, it had inherited from Britain the territories and borders formerly agreed by successive British and Afghan governments since 1893, a view supported by the British Government in 1950. So the Durand Line remained, and still so remains, the political border between Pakistan and Afghanistan.

Notwithstanding the declared allegiance to Pakistan of the tribes between the Line and the administrative border, and the fact that they and the rulers of the new state were co-religionists, the loose form of control as practised by the British continued and the tribes remained untrammelled by state bureaucracy. In 1944 a British committee set up to review future defence policy on the Frontier recommended a return to the Curzon plan whereby all regular forces would be withdrawn from tribal territory

176

Farewell to the Frontier. Razmak Camp at the time of the British evacuation in 1947.

into cantonments along the administrative border, while the unadministered districts would again become the responsibility of the Militias, or Scouts as they were known; the latter, however, would be better equipped so that calls for further assistance would be lessened. After partition Pakistan adopted this plan which was carried out without mishap, except for some minor trouble in North Waziristan, inspired by the Fakir of Ipi who, in alliance with Abdul Ghaffar Khan, had remained hostile to the creation of Pakistan, and would continue to be a thorn in the side of the new state until his death in 1960.

Thus, after 1947, British troops were seen no more in the Frontier hills and passes. But here and there along the Khyber Pass, whose name perhaps most symbolizes the Frontier, are carved in the rock memorials of the men who, when the politicians and administrators had done their best, or worst, were called upon, so many times, to hold the line in these unchanging hills, memorials of those who will not come again: the badges of the regiments that passed this way. Many of these belong to regiments of the old Indian Army, Sikhs, Punjabis, Gurkhas, Frontier Force, Baluchis, whose traditions are carried on in the new armies of India and Pakistan. Others are those of the old regiments of the British Line: Fusiliers, Highlanders, Rifles, Irish and Welsh, and the county regiments of England: Cheshires, Borders, Dorsets and many others. One, that of the Essex Regiment, has in a way a special significance, carved as it is in the very pass which years before its forebears of the 44th Foot were striving to reach, when they died some seventy miles to the west upon the hill of Gandamak, and the North-West Frontier of India first began to grip the British imagination.

Appendix

Chronological Table of North-West Frontier Campaigns

1849	Baizais	1879	Zakha Khel
1850	Kohat Afridis	1880	Marris
1851	Mohmands	1881	Mahsuds
1852	Ranizais	1883	Shiranis
1852	Utman Khel	1888	Black Mountain Tribes
1852	Waziris	1890	Zhob Valley
1852	Black Mountain Tribes	1891	Black Mountain Tribes
1853	Hindustani Fanatics	1891	Miranzai
1853	Shiranis	1891	Hunza and Nagir
1853	Kohat Afridis	1894	Mahsuds
1854	Mohmands	1895	Chitral
1854	Afridis	1897	Tochi Wazirs
1855	Orakzais	1897	Malakand
1855	Miranzai	1897	Mohmands
1856	Kurram	1897	Orakzais
1857	Bozdars	1897	Afridis
1857	Hindustani Fanatics	1900	Mahsuds
1859	Waziris	1908	Zakha Khel
1860	Mahsuds	1908	Mohmands
1863	Ambela	1915	Mohmands
1863	Mohmands	1917	Mahsuds
1868	Black Mountain Tribes	1919–20	Waziristan
1868	Bizotis	1923	Mahsuds
1872	Tochi	1927	Mohmands
1877	Jowakis	1930–31	Afridis
1878	Utman Khel	1933	Mohmands
1878	Zakha Khel	1935	Mohmands
1878	Mohmands	1936–37	Waziristan
1878	Zaimukhts	1937–39	Waziristan

Campaign Medals

1. Only four Indian General Service medals were issued for the Frontier campaigns, though with various clasps for individual expeditions:

a. **1854–1895**
    Ribbon red, blue, red, blue, red. First clasp issued retrospectively in 1869 for expeditions back to 1849.
b. **1895–1902**
    Ribbon red, green, red, green, red.

c. 1908–1935
Ribbon dark blue edged green.
d. 1936–1939
Ribbon stone-colour, edged green and red.

2. Separate medals were issued for the first two Afghan Wars, as follows:

a. First Afghan War
i. Capture of Ghazni, 1839. Ribbon half red, half green.
ii. Individual medals for: Kandahar 1842; Ghazni-Kabul 1842; Kandahar-Ghazni-Kabul 1842; Kabul 1842; Kalat-i-Gilzai 1842; Jalalabad 1842 (two types).
All ribbons watered rainbow pattern.

b. Second Afghan War
i. One medal with clasps for: Ali Masjid; Peiwar Kotal; Charasia; Kabul; Ahmad Khel; Kandahar. Ribbon green, edged red.
ii. Star for Roberts' march from Kabul to Kandahar. Ribbon as in 2.a.ii above.

3. The Third Afghan War was covered by a clasp to the 1908–1935 Indian General Service medal.

Battle Honours

The following were awarded to British and Indian regiments:

Afghanistan	Frontier
AFGHANISTAN	CHITRAL
GHUZNEE (Ghazni)	DEFENCE OF CHITRAL
KHELAT (Kalat)	PUNJAB FRONTIER
JELLALABAD (Jalalabad)	MALAKAND
CABOOL 1842 (Kabul)	SAMANA
KHELAT-I-GHILZIE (Kalat-i-Ghilzai)	TIRAH
KANDAHAR 1842	N. W. FRONTIER (various dates, 1914–18)
	BALUCHISTAN 1918
AFGHANISTAN 1878–80	
ALI MASJID	
PEIWAR KOTAL	
CHARASIA	
KABUL 1879	
AHMAD KHEL	
KANDAHAR 1880	
AFGHANISTAN 1919	

Glossary

Akhond   a religious teacher.
Dafadar   Indian cavalry sergeant.
Fakir   a holy man.
Ghazi   a fighter for the Faith.
Havildar   Indian infantry sergeant.
Jehad   a holy war.
Jemadar   Junior Indian cavalry troop or infantry company officer.
Jezail   a long musket.
Jirga   an assembly of tribal elders or representatives.
Kotal   a pass.
Lashkar   a tribal army.
Malik   a headman.
Mullah   a religious teacher or leader.
Naik   Indian corporal.
Nullah   a small valley or ravine.
Poshteen   a sheepskin coat with fleece worn inside.
Puggaree   a length of material, hence turban.
Ressaldar   Indian cavalry troop officer.
Ressaldar-Major   Senior Indian officer of a cavalry regiment.
Sangar   a stone breastwork.
Sepoy   Indian infantry private.
Silladar   Indian cavalryman providing own horse and equipment.
Sowar   Indian cavalry trooper.
Subedar   Indian infantry company officer.
Subedar-Major   Senior Indian officer of an infantry battalion.
Tulwar   a sabre.

Select Bibliography

There is a large amount of literature on the subject of the North-West Frontier. This list includes those works which have proved most useful in the compilation of this book.

Bruce, George, *Six Battles for India*, Arthur Barker, 1969.
The Cambridge History of India, Volume 6, Cambridge University Press, 1932.
Caroe, Olaf, *The Pathans, 550 BC–AD 1957*, Macmillan, 1958.
Cole, Major D. H., *Imperial Military Geography*, Sifton Praed, 1933.
Edwardes, Michael, *Playing the Great Game*, Hamish Hamilton, 1975.
Elliot, Major-General J. G., *The Frontier 1839–1947*, Cassell, 1968.

Forbes, Archibald, *The Afghan Wars, 1839–42* and *1878–80*, Seeley, 1892.

Forrest, G. W., *The Life of Sir Neville Chamberlain*, Blackwood, 1909.

Grant, James, *British Battles on Land and Sea*, Cassell, n.d.

Hamilton, General Sir Ian, *Listening for the Drums*, Faber, 1944.

Hanna, Colonel H. B., *The Second Afghan War*, Constable, 1910.

Harris, John, *Much Sounding of Bugles: The Siege of Chitral* 1895, Hutchinson, 1975.

Heathcote, T. A., *The Indian Army: The Garrison of British Imperial India, 1822–1922*, David & Charles, 1974.

–– *The Afghan Wars 1839–1919*. Osprey, 1980.

Hensman, Howard, *The Afghan War 1879–80*, W. H. Allen, 1881.

Hutchinson, Colonel H. D., *The Campaign in Tirah*, Macmillan, 1898.

Lambrick, H. T., *John Jacob of Jacobabad*, Cassell, 1960.

Lumsden, General Sir Peter & Elsmie, George, *Lumsden of the Guides*, John Murray, 1899.

Macrory, Patrick, *Signal Catastrophe: The Retreat From Kabul 1842*, Hodder and Stoughton 1966.

MacMunn, Lieutenant-General Sir George, *The Romance of the Indian Frontiers*, Jonathan Cape, 1931.

Mason, Philip, *A Matter of Honour: The Indian Army, its Officers and Men*, Jonathan Cape, 1974.

Masters, John, *Bugles and a Tiger*, Michael Joseph, 1956.

Maxwell, Leigh, *My God — Maiwand!*, Leo Cooper, 1979.

Miller, Charles, *Khyber*, Macdonald and Jane's, 1977.

Nevill, Captain H. L., *Campaigns on the North-West Frontier*, John Murray, 1912.

Roberts, Field-Marshal Lord, *Forty One Years in India*, Macmillan, 1898.

Swinson, Arthur, *North-West Frontier*, Hutchinson, 1967.

The Second Afghan War — Official Account, Army Headquarters, India, 1908.

Williamson, James, *A Short History of British Expansion*, Macmillan, 1931.

Woods, Frederick (Ed.), *Young Winston's Wars: Original Despatches of Winston. S. Churchill, 1897–1900*, Leo Cooper, 1972.

Younghusband, G. J., *Indian Frontier Warfare*, Kegan Paul, 1898.

–– *The Story of the Guides*, Macmillan, 1908.

Various Regimental Histories.

Periodicals

The British Empire (1972)

The Illustrated London News

The Illustrated Naval And Military Magazine (1884–85)

The Journal of the Society for Army Historical Research (1922–81)

The Navy and Army Illustrated (1895–1902)

Soldiers of the Queen: Journal of the Victorian Military Society (1974–81)

Wings (Orbis Publishing, partwork)

Various Regimental Journals.

Index